METHOD ACTING FOR WRITERS

LEARN DEEP POINT OF VIEW USING EMOTIONAL LAYERS

LISA HALL-WILSON

https://lisahallwilson.com

lisa@lisahallwilson.com

Method Acting For Writers: Learn Deep Point Of View Using Emotional Layers/ Lisa Hall-Wilson – First Edition

ISBN 978-0-9953238-2-7

INTRODUCTION

What Deep Point Of View Can Do For Your Writing

Are you struggling to create characters readers care about? Critique partners, editors or agents telling you to dig deeper emotionally? Do you want to write emotional arcs into your stories to keep readers engaged and turning the pages?

Deep point of view (POV) is dynamic, visceral, and immediate. The goal of this writing technique is for the writer to disappear and minimize the perceived distance between the reader and the point of view character (POVC). At the heart of deep POV is an immersive experience for the reader through an emotional connection to the character. Think of it like handing your reader a virtual reality headset. THAT's how close to the action your readers want to be.

This intimate and emotive style of writing resonates with contemporary readers if you've got the guts to "go there" with your characters. This book will explore the ultimate write-what-you-know principle. These aren't difficult skills to master, but this requires a shift in how you tell stories and sometimes those shifts don't seem intuitive.

Why Deep Point Of View?

In the early 2000s, I began to notice my favorite writers using a technique that pulled me deeper into stories than ever before. There had always been books I couldn't put down, but the frequency with which I encountered them increased exponentially. I was fascinated and did some digging. At that time, this technique was called close third person or some variation of that.

There wasn't much information out there about this technique, but the more I read the more I picked up intuitively. Fast forward five or ten years and this technique has a name: deep point of view. There are free and paid resources out there, but many cover the same basic foundational steps of this writing style making it really hard to leap frog from intermediate to advanced. It's really hard to take your writing to the next level when you don't know what you need to learn next.

I've spent ten years going to conferences and taking workshops, reading blogs and books, talking to published authors, paying for critiques, and paying professional editors to look at my work in order to learn deep point of view. I could only ever get one small step ahead at a time. It was frustrating to be told I still didn't have all the pieces over and over, and never knew which pieces I was missing.

This book is the result of an online class I've taught for a few years about writing in deep POV. I have a teacher's heart, so I'm always breaking things down to make it easier to share and teach. My goal is to equip those taking my class and get them back to writing FAST! I'd rather spend my time writing than learning about writing—maybe you're like me. I want the information hard and fast.

This book is a deep dive into deep POV. Over the years, my students have helped me hone and clarify the lessons and suggest where additional teaching was needed. I continue to coach many of them online.

This book aims to give you the reasoning behind many of the stylistic choices of deep POV so you'll know when to use these techniques in each of your stories, when not to use them, and how to use them to achieve specific goals or effects. This is a technique I'm passionate about, so I'm always blogging about the new things I'm learning or breaking things down for readers in a way that's easier to understand.

This book will cover the foundational building blocks necessary for this writing technique, but then I dive deep into the stylistic choices that can really take your writing to the next level so your stories grab readers by the throat and won't let go.

Let's dive deep and go beyond basics!!

LIMIT PERCEIVED DISTANCE BETWEEN READERS AND CHARACTERS

The goal of deep POV is to create an immersive and immediate reading experience. To create this effect, we need to eliminate any words or phrases that remind the reader they're a spectator or observer who's outside the story. Deep POV is about making intentional style choices to create that fictive dream.

Create Immediacy By Writing In Real Time

We want readers to feel like they're in the action *as it's happening*. This is achieved by writing as if the POVC is experiencing an event or conflict in real time. I'm not talking about flashbacks. Deep POV can be used equally with either past or present tense, first or third person POV (though the genre you're writing in may influence your choice. YA, for instance, often features first person POVCs). Don't write about events that have already taken place, instead write the scene as the character moves through it.

Joe ran up the stairs and threw open the door to Sally's bedroom. He couldn't believe what he saw. He ran back down the stairs and out to his truck. He had to stop her.

Readers want to see what Joe saw, understand the implications of what he sees AS Joe realizes it himself. They want to know how he feels about this, what's he afraid of? Why does this cause him to run for his truck? The way it's written above there's no urgency. There's nothing to cause the readers to lean in and feel Joe's tension.

Each time you remind readers that no matter what's about to happen your character is fine, then whatever trouble they get into won't have readers leaning forward in anticipation or surprise. You won't be able to create a sense of fear or dread or betrayal if the reader knows it's all going to be alright.

It all worked out for the best, but fear had coiled in her belly like a writhing snake.

Instead, take the reader on their own emotional journey as they work through the story alongside your characters. The reader wants to squirm, cringe, have their belly cramp because they don't know how this is going to turn out. They want to FEEL something. This is done with stylistic choices. The POVC's emotions and internal dialogue must convey an immediate sense of tension, uncertainty, fear—whatever it is, in a way that the reader perceives it's happening right now. Avoid summarizing, skimming over, or offering narration that will undermine the tension.

I'd read the article and my stomach churned in response.

This would be more powerful if the reader was aware of what caused the character such turmoil, but as it's written the painful part is already over. There's no reason to lean in. Instead of summarizing an event, take the reader through it.

I reread the date on the article three times. How had I missed this? Brian? My hand covered my throat. No. I don't believe it. Murder?

In the rewrite, the tension is more evident and the POVC's confusion is clear. The action is immediate and the reader knows everything the POVC does. Let's try another example:

Shawn walked through the house, shocked at what he saw. His mother's journal had been destroyed.

What did he see? Why was it shocking? What does shocking look like to Shawn and what can that tell us about his character?

Shawn searched each room for his mother's journal. There, on a side table, the familiar pink book cover stood out in the drab room. He picked up the book and ran his finger over the coffee stain rings marking the cover. His mother's gold foil name had been scratched out with a pen. His throat constricted. Who could desecrate a book like that?

Whether or not you agree that this qualifies as destroying a book doesn't matter, it does to this character. A reader will take that information and make a number of inferences about this character like what's important to Shawn and what motivates him. The reader's job is to make these decisions. Trust your reader to figure it out.

Distance Red Flags

There are some words that automatically create distance for readers and relegate them back into the theater seats watching the action. Do a search in your manuscript for some of these words and see how many you find (these are past tense, switch to present tense if that's what you're writing in):

watched, saw, felt, wished, heard, thought, made, caused, hoped, knew, wondered, remembered, wanted, believed, regarded, noticed, looked, smelled, realized, decided.

Obviously, this is not an exhaustive list of words and it would be unrealistic to think you could eliminate all of these words. These words don't always create distance, it will depend on context, but I've found these often tattle on telling in deep POV. Deep POV is the ultimate show don't tell writing technique. In the example below, can you see how these red flag words force the reader out of the story (italics used to identify distance words)?

With Distance: Jason *watched* the woman walk into the bar, her heels clicking on the hard linoleum. The lanky blond-from-a-box strode across the room towards the bar. Little early in the day for that much cleavage, *he thought*. He tipped his beer to his lips. But who was he to judge.

Without Distance: Feminine heels clicked on the hard linoleum behind him. Jason swiveled in his seat. The lanky blond-from-a-box strode across the room towards the bar. Little early in the day for that much cleavage. He tipped his beer to his lips. But who was he to judge.

Do you see how the internal dialogue seamlessly fits into the narrative? You didn't need me to 'tell' you which was narrative and which internal dialogue. I didn't need to put the internal dialogue in italics. I used sound to hint to the POVC that it was a woman walking into the bar. I don't need to 'tell' the reader that the POVC is seeing or watching. Limiting distance may require writing more words, but sometimes it's as easy as removing the distance words.

Distance Creeps In Through Sense and Thinking Words

We writers get subtle and add in distance in sneaky ways. The narrative must be written as though it's come directly from within the character's mind (first or third person doesn't matter). With sense words, there's power in specificity. Instead of saying there's a smell, a noise, or something is beautiful, show readers what the character is smelling, hearing, or seeing. Let readers see it through the eyes of the POVC.

Internal dialogue must not be written as though there's an invisible audience. When we post on Facebook, we write with the assumption of an invisible audience. Don't write internal dialogue as though it's for the reader's benefit.

He remembered they vacationed at this cottage as a kid becomes – They'd vacationed here.

Steve was sure she could climb the ladder becomes – She could climb the ladder. (Steve is the POVC.)

The kitchen smelled amazing becomes — She leaned over the pan of hot rolls and breathed in the buttery cinnamon scent.

There are some instances where you might choose to write in a shallower point of view strategically to create a specific effect, but we'll get to that in a bit.

THE READER'S COURTROOM

When writing in deep POV, think of yourself as a lawyer in a court case. Your job is to present evidence to the judge (the reader) about who your character is, what's important to them, their story goals, and why they behave and think the way they do. The array of evidence you have available to you to prove your case is everything your POVC knows, thinks, tastes, touches, hears, sees, etc. But that's all you have.

In deep POV, telling is avoided at all costs. Some stylistic choices that are acceptable in shallower POVs is considered telling in deep POV.

One of the most foundational aspects of writing in deep POV is to avoid naming emotions: love, hate, frustration, lust, grief, envy, etc. Once you label what your POVC is feeling for the judge (the reader), you've taken them off the bench and put them in gallery with the noisy journalists. A judge doesn't enter a courtroom for a show, to be entertained, they expect to be put to work. Instead, provide evidence to the judge (the reader) about why the character is saying, thinking, doing, and the judge hands down a verdict on what the character feels.

Most intermediate writers understand show don't tell. What they struggle with is trusting their readers to figure it out, so they show AND tell. The judge (the reader) must be trusted to figure out what your POVC is experiencing, they want to be put to work. A bored judge checks out and finds a bookmark.

Shane walked with his hands in his pockets and kicked a can down the street. Depressed, he didn't want to go home. "Nobody would miss me anyway."

This is an example of showing and telling. I could eliminate the telling phrase from the example above, to only provide evidence about how Shane feels, and you could figure it out well enough without being told.

Shane walked with his hands in his pockets and kicked a can down the street. "Nobody would miss me anyway."

The second one made you think, just a little. That's the goal. The reader wants to be put to work; they want to dive into the story and experience everything the POVC experiences in real time like you've handed them a virtual reality headset.

I've put the named emotions in bold below so you can easily see what I'm talking about.

Perplexed, *Sally sank down to the sofa to think.* (telling - what does perplexed look like to this character?)

Sally slouched into the sofa cushions and threw her hands up. What now?

Megan waved ***nervously*** *and giggled.* (telling - what does this character do when she's nervous?)

Megan waved and giggled. Too much. She pulled her hand behind her back. Maybe he hadn't seen her?

***Rage** coursed through Warren, his fists clenched at his sides.*
(telling - what does rage do to this character?)

Warren's heart pounded in his throat and his face heated til his cheeks were on fire. He had to do something. Now.

Don't Keep Secrets

The POVC can't keep secrets from the reader. The reader wants to discover things as the POVC does. The reader is firmly planted inside the POVC's head so there can't be any secrets between them. If your POVC knows who's approaching them then the reader should know. If the POVC knows what's behind the spooky door, the reader has to know. You must build in tension and surprise through what the POVC doesn't know, has misunderstood, doesn't see coming, whatever.

This is not the same as an unreliable narrator. An unreliable narrator tells the reader the truth *as they know it.* Even unreliable narrators must tell the truth, their truth.

"My other friends are in music relaxation class, which I do not attend, because smooth jazz makes me angry sometimes."
Matthew Quick, *Silver Linings Playbook*

It's clear from the quote above that Pat, the POVC, has a couple of issues, right. He's walked out of the bad place with his mother, and he's explained that the bad place steals his memory and it's filled with doctors and nurses, roommates who drool and don't talk, and paper cups filled with pills. Pat doesn't need to *tell* us that the bad place is a psychiatric facility of some kind, we can take the evidence presented and make that conclusion ourselves.

Pat doesn't need to tell us that his version of reality, that how he perceives the world around him, isn't quite the whole truth.

It's the truth as he sees it, and that's a really important distinction. We know from even this small snippet, that we can't trust that things are the way Pat thinks they are.

Emotions Are Subjective

The other big problem with labeling an emotion for readers in deep point of view is that emotions are subjective. What's torture for one character is just every day for another. Love to one character is infatuation to another. It's better to show what these emotions feel like and what they cause the character to do, in order to help readers understand why the POVC is making that choice, thinking that, saying that, behaving in that way.

Let's look at an example.

Love flooded Steve's chest every time he looked at Melissa.

What does 'love' feel like to Steve? Is he floating or drowning? Is he ecstatic or terrified? What does Steve consider love to be? Is it really love or is it lust or just attraction? Does he love Melissa romantically, or has she just saved his butt at work? Is Steve even aware that he feels this way—is this author intrusion? You see how 'love flooded his chest' is drawing a conclusion for the reader? Provide evidence of what's going on in Steve's head so readers understand he's in love (even if he doesn't yet know it himself), and show readers what Steve finds attractive, what he values, what he's missing.

Let's have another try at why Steve loves Melissa.

Steve shook his head and smiled at the over-filled backpack Melissa wore, likely filled with every textbook assigned to every class, and more paper and pens than she could ever need. She turned, scanned the room, and then shot up to her tiptoes and waved at him. His chest filled with warmth. The heat spread through his whole body until sweat broke out on his brow. Didn't she know he'd been watching for her? He'd always look for her until she was beside him again.

Steve could've commented on Melissa's hair or body, on how smart she is, how she fills in the gaps where his own introversion and social awkwardness work against him ... I could continue coming up theories. This is what love looks and feels like TO STEVE.

Knowing why Steve loves Melissa shows readers what's important to him, how he values others, the gaps or weaknesses in his own character he's looking to shore up in a partner, etc. Readers see what's important to Melissa through what Steve is drawn to. Answering the WHY question helps the reader cheer for Steve.

Do the hard work of exploring what each emotion feels or looks like instead of drawing a conclusion and telling the reader what's going on.

ANSWER THE WHY!

If we understand that the goal of deep POV is to hand readers a virtual reality headset so that they're experiencing the story with the POVC, in real time, and that we must eliminate as much telling as possible and instead present evidence to the reader, the next question should be how? Stephen King in his book *On Writing* talks about the writer's toolbox. What tools do we have in the deep POV toolbox to use as evidence for the reader/judge?

- Internal Dialogue (thoughts)
- Body Language (facial expressions, gestures, posture, tone of voice)
- Spoken Dialogue (both from the POVC and other characters)
- Physiology (what's going on internally: heart rate, sweating, etc.)
- Behavior

Readers want to take an emotional journey alongside the

main character in every scene. Not enough evidence and the reader is lost, too much and the reader is bored.

To effectively write in deep POV, the reader (and author) must know the WHY for the entire novel, each act, and each scene. I find it helps to break it down in that way, you may want to go even more granular. Why did your POVC say that, do that, hide that, run away or stand and fight—all of it.

The WHY must be specific to that character in that moment. The WHY should give the reader insight into the POVC's motives, their character, their priorities, and their passions.

Drill Down Into The Heart Of The WHY

If you're more inclined to plan before you begin writing, knowing the WHY may be more intuitive for you. For those who are pantsers (like me), getting into the habit of knowing the WHY is often tackled on rewrites. The key to drilling down into motivations and goals is to keep asking why.

Why is this character choosing the hard thing, why are they standing up when they don't have to, why are they fighting when it's easier to walk away? Drill down to the very heart of the issue for this character. Whether you need a chart and time line, or simply need to make some jotted sketches, the method isn't important. Keep asking why until you have found the root of the question.

Let's consider Skeeter from the bestselling book *The Help*. Why does Skeeter order books blacklisted by the state of Mississippi? She's rebellious. That's not why. That's a consequence of why. Why?

She feels powerless to change or correct the injustice of segregation. Why?

Her family participated in the injustice, the inequality. She feels guilty. Why?

Her family employed an African-American servant and so she sees herself as part of the problem—she doesn't deserve the privileges being born White has given her. Now we're getting somewhere. Action.

She's going to write about the situation and give a voice to those no one listens to. She wants to change things and use the privilege she enjoys to do it. THIS is Skeeter's motivation, this is what she desires, and these passions and past experience will be the filter through which she relates the story to readers.

That's the WHY on a story level. Let's look at the WHY at a scene level from Patricia Briggs' novel *Cry Wolf*.

"The Marrock's business apparently concluded, the other two wolves surged past Anna, George deliberately bumping against her. She pulled back from him and instinctively wrapped her arms protectively around herself. He gave her a sneer he hid quickly from the others.

'*Illegitimis nil carborundum,*' she murmured. It was stupid. She knew it even before George's fist struck out."

Anna is the POVC in this scene. What evidence do we have of her emotions? She's bumped, she perceives deliberately, and pulls back instinctively protecting herself. What emotions do we have evidence for to give us the WHY of her actions? Fear with a good dose of anticipation or dread. That triggers her fight, flight or freeze instinct. She can't escape and wrestling with someone bigger than her has proven pointless (we know that from earlier in the scene). But she's still fighting in her own way. The Latin phrase is her own private rebellion. Her own way to regain control in a situation where she feels she has no control.

So, the WHY in this scene—why does she rebel? To feel like she still has some measure of control. What did she say in Latin? Don't let the bastards grind you down. We'll get more into primary emotions and secondary emotions in a bit.

The Why Is Not A Fish Head

I first read this term on Kristen Lamb's blog. The fish head refers to all the backstory we know about our characters. Where they grew up, who their best friend was in sixth grade, why they got fired from their first job—all of it. This WHY is important for you to know, but if it doesn't directly influence the action of the plot the reader doesn't need to know it. It's important sometimes to know all this to get to know your characters, but readers only want to enjoy the fruit of your labor. What do you do with a fish head? You cut it off, right. It's not digestible.

Backstory is not necessarily what I mean by knowing the WHY. You need to understand motivations and goals and how those influence the current action in the story.

Joe is in love with Emily. She's the prettiest girl he's ever seen, she thinks he's funny, and she doesn't care that he has a dead-end job at a factory. But Joe can't bring himself to ask her to marry him. This WHY is important for readers to know.

Why does Joe pull away emotionally when Emily asks him about getting married? He doesn't think he's good enough for her. The WHY we're concerned with is which emotions this self-belief brings up and what Joe does with them. Some additional WHY may be that Joe's parents split when he was young and he's hesitant to enter into a relationship that isn't guaranteed to work out. This may or may not come out in this scene.

Why Joe's father left may not be relevant in this scene. Why Joe was there to watch it happen may not be relevant. That Joe was standing outside the house on the sidewalk on a hot summer day while his ice cream cone melted at his feet when his father walked out on them is definitely not relevant for readers. Those things have influenced and shaped Joe, but unless they directly influence this scene with Emily, the reader doesn't need to know it right now. It's a fish head. Cut it out.

FOUR LAYERS OF EMOTIONS

We need to take a page from psychology and understand how emotions work to really make deep POV work for your story. We want to avoid telling or drawing conclusions for readers and instead present evidence. To that end, we need to recognize that emotions are messy. They're often blurred, spill into and conflict with each other, and only very self-aware personalities are able to wade into the mire and label each emotion they're feeling. Let's recap quickly. In deep POV, we avoid naming emotions as much as possible.

She waved *anxiously*.

Rage coursed through him.

He slammed the door, *frustration* making his fists clench.

Our brains process emotions in two steps. We feel and experience emotions on one side of our brain, but the labeling, processing, and analyzing of emotions happens on the other side. That's why you can be mad and not be able to articulate why immediately. You can feel pent up and restless and not know why.

Some people never learn to label and analyze how they feel. Instead, they run, hide, or numb their emotions through alcohol or other substances, work, busyness, sex, porn...

Emotions happen in layers, and when writing deep point of view knowing this helps to break down the WHY of any scene or emotion.

Primary Emotions

Primary emotions are instinctual, unthinking, primal emotions. These emotions are the gut reactions. The range of emotions available to us hasn't changed over time, but the societies and traditions we live in can dictate how those emotions are labeled, expressed, and suppressed. You are capable of feeling one or a dozen primary emotions at once. Some examples of primary emotions are: fear, joy, sadness, disappointment, helplessness, hopelessness, despair, betrayal, frustration, grief, lust, and attraction.

Most often, we show readers primary emotions through body language and physiology—what's going on inside such as heart rate, skin prickles, and sweating.

If you're a parent, consider those first few days with your first baby. You probably cycled through fear, frustration, love, doubt, and joy all in a twenty-four-hour period. Emotions overlap, they crash into one another. Some of those emotions made you feel good, others perhaps made you judge or doubt yourself. When strong primary emotions get hold of us, we are uncomfortable, out of control. No one likes these feelings, so we DO something to bring comfort or regain control.

Emotional Triggers

Triggers are a learned response to strong primary emotions

that catapult us to a behavior to relieve the discomfort we feel. For victims of abuse, a trigger might be a phrase their abuser used, a smell, or a place. For a perfectionist, getting a stain on their blouse at lunch could be a trigger for shame and your POVC is immediately frantic to remove the stain. For a man who never felt he measured up to his father's expectations, that shame or anger could be triggered whenever he perceives he's failed at something. To gain control, to get out from under the shame, he screams at his wife and kids. Now he's in control again.

With emotional triggers, instead of logically working through the emotions being felt and dismissing the ones that aren't valid, we're instantly reacting in a learned pattern. We're not aware of the primary emotions involved, we act on the secondary emotion. Emotional triggers are very difficult to overcome and require enough self-awareness to dig down into the primary emotions behind them. (The hardest part of any therapy session.) This could be a great emotional arc to give your character if they have to overcome something from their past that's become an emotional trigger for them.

Triggers are most often shown to readers through internal dialogue.

Secondary Emotions

Secondary emotions are our thinking reactions to primary emotions. Anger, shame, anxiety, grief, love, hate—these are all secondary emotions. A secondary emotion is made up of or fed by one or a few primary emotions, and the mix will be very individual and specific to each character and situation. For example, anger is rarely an unthinking primitive emotional response. Anger is a reaction to being frustrated, scared, relieved, betrayed, etc.

Let's pause here for a moment because I've had students stumble over this concept. Anger is a reaction to primary emotions like fear, surprise, and betrayal. The primary emotions are what's felt, but the secondary emotion is often what's observed. Love is a reaction to attraction, lust, and happiness (not a definitive list). Hate is a response to dislike, fear, or pain. This blend of primary emotions will be unique for each character in each scene.

Emotions are not simple and straight forward. Not only do primary emotions blend and mix, secondary emotions add to the complexity so this is an additional layer of emotional turmoil or conflict you can add. Your ability to show the reader that blend of emotions will result in a richer emotional journey for the reader.

In order to realistically show a secondary emotion, you must know the primary emotions fueling it. Anger fueled by fear and surprise will look different, have a different goal, than someone who's been rejected and hurt.

Now that we've mapped out the beginning layers, now that we know the WHY, we're able to present evidence to our readers so that even irrational or disproportionate actions make sense. The reader doesn't necessarily have to agree with the character's choices, but they do have to understand them. The character can lie to themselves, but they can't lie to the reader. It must be clear to the reader what's actually going on.

External Reactions — Behavior

This fourth layer is the observable part of primary and secondary emotions. Primary emotions compel us to DO something, and if we can't resolve the emotion in question we'll often seek to regain control of our emotions. Fear and surprise force a character to run away or fight back. Love forces them to hug or kiss.

Where observable reactions serve us well is that we can have other characters comment on or react to the behavior. *What's the matter with you? What are you so angry about?* Whether the POVC acknowledges they're behaving erratically or illogically doesn't matter as long as you tip off the reader that's what's going on. Show your POVC over reacting and if readers understand the WHY they'll stick with your character even if (or even because) they're floundering.

In any given scene, your POVC could experience one or all of these emotional layers. Each layer may only be a sentence. Just a word. *Run!* But readers will be pulled deeper into the story this way and take their own emotional journey. The emotional journey for readers may not be the same emotional journey as your POVC, but that's OK. Your goal is to make the reader feel tension, apprehension, surprise without telling them your character is mad, happy, angry, or full of shame.

Here's a real-life example of how the reader can know what's going on, can label an emotion, even if the POVC or other characters aren't able to. I interviewed a Canadian nurse years ago for an article and she shared the following story with me. (I'm paraphrasing her story, these aren't her words.) The nurse was working in Cambodia as a missionary providing basic health exams to women in slums.

The nurse waved to the next woman in line to come forward. The nurse smiled and through an interpreter asked how she could help.

The Cambodian woman placed a hand over her chest. She told the interpreter she was having chest pains. Had been having chest pains for years. Her expression never changed but there was a flutter in her hand and she stared at the nurse with focused intensity.

The nurse frowned. "That's not good." She listens to the woman's heart and checked her pulse but found everything within normal ranges. She did a physical exam but there was nothing abnormal. There didn't appear to be anything wrong. The nurse asked the woman if the pains got worse if she was tired or had been working hard? Did the pains get worse when she ate or didn't eat?

No.

Stumped, the nurse glanced around the room at the other women gathered along the wall and out the door waiting to see her. None of them smiled or frowned. In fact, like the woman in front of her they didn't show any emotion at all. She turned to the interpreter. "Why do all these women sit there like that, no expressions?"

He leaned in. "Because of the Khmer Rouge. If you showed any emotion, they punished you more."

The nurse shut down the churning in her gut and focused on her patient again. Getting upset wouldn't help these people. Was the pain physical? "When your chest hurts, what goes through your mind? Are you thinking about anything in particular?"

The woman glanced between the nurse and the interpreter. She nodded slowly and spoke a few words. Her expression didn't change at all like it was cast in stone.

The interpreter's expression softened. His translation had been monotone and without expression the whole day, like he was bored, but now his tone grew deeper. "My baby, she says. My chest hurts when I think about my baby." He leaned in. "Her baby was killed in front of her by the Khmer Rouge many years ago."

The nurse nodded her thanks. An ache spread through her own chest and she swallowed the lump in her throat. That explained the chest pains.

Now, can you guess, based on the evidence presented, what emotion the Cambodian woman in this story is experiencing? This woman had no word for grief because that emotion wasn't expressed or acknowledged in her community/society. The nurse had to explain what grief was and that the symptoms being experienced weren't caused by any physical ailment.

Even if your character can't or won't acknowledge how they feel, their body language, tone of voice, behavior, internal dialogue and/or physiology will provide the necessary evidence for readers to make a decision on what emotion(s) is at play.

BLENDING EMOTIONAL LAYERS

Now, what many newer writers misunderstand about deep POV is that each emotional layer overlaps and is interconnected. These emotions and actions are not felt in isolation of one another. It's like a spider's web. Every intersection of the web is influenced by every other intersection. A tremor in a far corner of the web is felt throughout, right. Don't strive for strict delineation between the layers, let them overlap and conflict with one another.

When you jump straight to the secondary emotion or the behavior, the reader doesn't understand the why question. Why is the character reacting like this? I don't mind reading unlikeable characters, or even characters who make bad decisions, but I have to understand why that reaction is rational to them. This is equally important for protagonists and antagonists if they're both POV characters.

When a character jumps straight to anger and skips over the WHY, readers are put back in the theater seats observing the action. These internal, subtle shifts from one emotion to another, the blending of emotions, helps draw the reader farther into the story. Let a character's thoughts conflict with their actions and dialogue. Let their thoughts conflict with what their body feels. Let them think one thing and act in a contrary way, but make sure the reader knows why.

Additionally, be sure that each action has consequences and that the consequences layer and build upon one another. One doesn't instantly get over heart break or recover overnight from a traumatic experience. Each of those events should have tugged the web and the reverberations may be felt for a long time afterwards.

What Does This Layering Look Like?

This is where the rubber meets the road. If our aim is to layer emotions but not end up with an ...and then, ...and then, ... and then... construction, how do we do it?

Primary Emotion

The first layer, the primary emotions, is where you begin. Which are the most prominent primary emotions in this scene for this character? Keep in mind what the story goal for that scene is and what's at stake for your POVC. What is the need they're working to fix; the problem they're trying to solve? Pick a scene from your WIP and jot down the scene goal, what's at stake for the character, and what their reaction to that obstacle is. Don't list just one primary emotion, give yourself a few minutes and dig a little deeper. Can you list five possible primary emotions this scene could generate?

Which emotion feels truest? Try to avoid being predictable. I've done hundreds of interviews with former addicts and prostitutes, church leaders, executives, accountants, entertainers, TV hosts, authors, musicians, and ordinary people. For my column, I began each interview by asking the same question and never got the same answer twice. Their answer always surprised me. Let your character's individual likes and dislikes, history and hopes influence the range of emotions they feel in any given situation.

The emotion you pick needs to be more intense than the others. Now, take on the role of a detective and dig into the evidence you need to prove your case to the reader. What do you have at hand to work with? You have the silent orchestra of body language (posture, facial expressions, gestures), physiology, and tone of voice. You have internal dialogue and spoken dialogue at hand also. Are there other characters in this scene who could make an observation about what they're seeing or interpreting?

(Tavia is the POVC below)

Her sister launched herself at the stranger and the impact forced him back a step. He caught her with one arm and kissed her. Not a kiss on the cheek in greeting, or even a chaste kiss between acquaintances. This was a kiss between lovers.

Tavia stared, open mouthed. What was going on? When had this happened? Tavia cleared her throat.

In this snippet, which primary emotions are at play? Tavia's observing her sister run to a stranger and they share a kiss, a passionate kiss. What's she feeling? Can you see the surprise, shock, confusion? You can guess at what she's feeling based on her body language and internal dialogue.

Triggers

Is there a trigger? Is there a perfect storm of emotions that will catapult your character into a reaction that's over the top or disproportionate to the situation? Ever been in that situation?

I had a friend in university whom I had given money to in order to buy concert tickets for us both and the tickets were misplaced on the night of the concert.

This person ran around their home turning over chairs and throwing sofa cushions on the floor in a blind panic. You'd have thought we had half an hour to find our passports and flee the country. The longer the search went on, the more frantic they became. Tears were shed. Finally, they flopped onto their sofa and threw up their hands. *I'm such an idiot, how could I lose those? Now I'll have to pay you back and I don't have the money to do that...*

They could articulate that the reaction wasn't proportionate to the situation, but they seemed powerless to stop the mental crazy train. That's a trigger. Can you guess secondary emotion was triggered? Shame. Guilt tells us we've done a bad thing, shame tells us we are bad.

Years later, I asked them what was going through their mind at that point—what really triggered the shame? (The shame was observable from their dialogue, body language, and agitation.) They remembered their father belittling them as a child and the message they recited to themselves was "you can't do anything right." What message is your character silently reciting? Is your character at war with themselves? This takes a good amount of personal reflection so there's lots of room here for character arc.

Secondary Emotions

Secondary emotions are the thinking response to primary emotions. The secondary emotion can conflict or be confirmed by the character's behavior.

The husband who's been passed over for a promotion comes

home and sits down to dinner. He lights into his wife about the food, it's too simple, not cooked enough, cooked too much, isn't to his taste. The wife can calmly watch the panic and then simply ask, "Did something happen at work?"

How will he react? Is that enough for him to acknowledge his misplaced anger or does he need to hold on to the anger to regain control of himself or get out from under shame or another secondary emotion? You see how complex it can get.

Aralyn turned. The shadows hid much of her expression. "Tavia, this is my Edric." The joy in her voice was clear.

My Edric? Tavia studied the stranger from boots to crown, what she could see in the dark. "This is the secret you've been keeping to yourself these last few months?" Aralyn nodded and hugged Edric's waist. Tavia's shoulders sagged just a little and her throat loosened enough to take a deep breath again. "I am glad it is a happy secret."

Her primary emotions were confusion, surprise, and shock. She cleared her throat, subtext for her sister to explain what was going on. Does the fact that Tavia waited for her sister to explain show you anything about her character? Her thinking reaction to the primary emotions is to study the man and evaluate the threat. She dismisses the threat and is flooded with relief. In this context, relief is a secondary emotion because it's her thinking response to the surprise, shock and confusion. Her shoulders sag and she takes a deep breath.

Once you have in mind what you want to accomplish with any scene, what the character's goals are, what's at stake, and what emotions are fueling the conflict, then you can apply art (that's in the chapters to follow). Find beta readers willing to share the honest truth with you about what emotions they pick up on so you know if you've scored or missed the goal posts.

Deep Dive Into Time And Emotions In Internal Dialogue

How we process emotions is very individual, but the passage of time affects how we talk and think about emotional trauma. If we go back to emotions being experienced and processed by different parts of the brain, the more time that passes the more objective and analytical we can be about how we are/were feeling.

Here's an example.

Sarah has just witnessed her beloved cat, Fluffy get hit by a car and killed. In the moment, she's in shock. She's overwhelmed with feelings of sadness, surprise, and pain. She isn't going to label any of those raw primary emotions though, she's just going to react. A neighbor helps her bury the cat and Sarah rushes into the house and calls her mom. She's crying, repeating herself, and not making a lot of sense. These emotions are uncomfortable and to displace the discomfort, to bring some order to the chaos, she needs TO DO SOMETHING. Calling her mom may bring enough of a sense of security to settle her emotions.

Maybe talking to her mom opens the floodgates to the emotions, but she doesn't have words to describe how she feels. Instead, in order to regain control of her emotions, her "thinking" response is to get angry. On the phone with her mom, she rails at the driver for not watching where he was going, maybe she blames the cat, or maybe she turns that anger inward and berates herself. She can't be trusted to own a pet, she's a terrible person.

We've got three layers of emotion there, right? We could ratchet up the tension even more by making Fluffy the second cat she's lost on the road and trigger all the old feelings like they've just happened all over again.

Now, the passage of time will affect how Sarah thinks about this traumatic event. After a week, Sarah's emotions will still be raw but she'll have her composure back. She'll use different words to talk about Fluffy. She may have gained some perspective though the anger may still linger. A month or so later, probably she'll have worked through the emotions from that night enough to ditch the anger and label her emotions as grief, shock, sadness, and begin to heal. Now when she talks to her mom, she could realistically say, "I'm just sad. I miss Fluffy."

The more time that passes after a traumatic emotional event, the more realistic it is to label the emotions that were felt. An exception to this would be post traumatic stress disorder where your body reacts as though the initial trauma is present even if the mind acknowledges there's no threat. Remember that part of the power of deep POV is immediacy, so if you need to bring up a past hurt make sure to share it with readers in a way that it directly effects the current conflict.

BODY LANGUAGE

Understanding body language and what it expresses is an important tool in the deep POV toolbox. How characters stand, their expressions, tone of voice and even volume are all common ways to show the emotional layers in any given scene.

Interpretation

Remember, your job is not to have your POVC simply report on what's going on around them. They must be the filter through which the reader experiences the story. The reader wants to know what the POVC thinks and feels about everything that's important to the story. It's important to interpret the body language for the reader through your character's lens and personality. Leave room for incorrect interpretations and miscommunication.

Eye contact, for instance, is very powerful depending on whether it's wanted. A young woman reading a book in a coffee shop notices a man watching her. If she doesn't want to be interrupted from her reading, if the eye contact isn't wanted, she might acknowledge and dismiss the eye contact, she might aggressively meet his gaze. She might do her best to act like she hasn't noticed. What feelings are triggered to cause each reaction? The man may interpret her disinterest as a signal to try harder and become more aggressive.

In the example below, see if you can identify the emotions involved.

One soldier bent and pulled the pin securing the lid, lifted the top and stepped back.

Her father's lifeless eyes stared up at the ceiling, his mouth gaped as if he'd died mid-scream. She coughed and sputtered like she'd been punched in the gut. Her hand covered her mouth and she dropped to her knees. Crawling the short distance, she reached for the box and then withdrew her fingers. There was no mistaking Wyne's features. But that wasn't her father anymore. Her fingers trembled and tears blurred her vision. She shut the box. How had this happened?

I see shock, grief, sadness, revulsion... But the primary emotions bump into one another. They overlap, they cause a chain reaction of shock after shock. She shuts the box. She's turned off the emotions. She can't deal with it all. It's too much. This scene required a lot of emotional trauma and upheaval, the emotions had to be overwhelming and chaotic.

Build In Qualifiers For Readers (Avoid POV Breaks)

In the above example, did you wonder if there was a POV break? How could the POVC know if her father died mid scream or not? Notice the built-in qualifier.

...his mouth gaped *as if* he'd died mid-scream.

One way to signal to the reader that the POVC is guessing

about or interpreting body language based on their own knowledge is to use conditional words: seems like, as if, appears to, etc.

Sheila sat at the bar. The man next to her started at her knees and let his gaze wander up her body ***as if*** *he was undressing her in his mind.*

There's more on this in the chapter on subtext when we discuss familiarity, past history, and other non-verbal cues that allow your POVC or other characters to interpret or guess at body language and what's being communicated.

METHOD ACTING FOR WRITERS

Our creative cousins in acting can teach us a few things through how they prepare for a role. They must step into another's skin and as novelists, we step into the minds of our characters. We can borrow a few acting techniques and adapt them to help us write more compelling characters.

Remember, deep POV is your POVC filtering the story through their own lens, interpreting everything for the reader. Here's where you literally put into practice write what you know.

What Is Emotional Memory?

Emotional memory is the idea of recalling an emotion you've felt previously. The range of emotions available to humans has not changed, what differs between people and cultures is the intensity, openness of expression, and acknowledgment of emotions. At some point, everyone's been betrayed, humiliated, scared, anxious, argumentative, frustrated, in love, envious, etc. We're going to tap into that with emotional memory.

What this means is that many of the emotions your character

experiences you've also likely experienced, even if it's to a different degree or was caused by a different scenario or event.

"I thought the drama was when actors cried. But drama is when the audience cries." Frank Capra

Every POVC in your story is you in some way. You are the villain, the hero and the sidekick. By lending emotional memory to your story, you can write with more authenticity explored through the unique lens and interpretations of your point of view characters.

Method actors are known for going to sometimes extreme lengths to prepare for a role. I'm not suggesting that you pursue method writing, as I've seen it called, to such extremes as experiencing everything your character does. But you can sit in your writing cave and recall the emotions you felt when you first asked a girl out on a date, the angst of starting a new school or job, or maybe the silent compassion of a pet when you were crying.

How Does Emotional Memory Work?

Think of a moment that's emotionally intense for your POVC. Determine what two or three emotions are powering the emotional tension in that scene (if it's earlier in the book maybe it's only one emotion). Have you experienced any of those emotions even if it wasn't as intense?

Think back to that time or moment. Find a quiet place and let your mind relive that moment. Force your mind to go blank, remain still, and let the memory well up like water filling a pool. Focus on how the emotion felt. What is your body doing, what body language are you using? Are you trying to hide your emotions?

Let's say your character is being chased through the woods by a serial killer. You've likely never had this experience (thankfully), but I bet at one point you've had to run farther than you trained for (even if you have to go back in your memory to that high school gym class). You know what it feels like to have your legs aching, heart banging inside your chest, throat seared with every breath.

You might not have been in a race for your life, but you've been scared before. I don't mean startled, but scared. Maybe you were lost for five minutes at the supermarket when you were seven, got lost in a sketchy part of town, or made rules about how to keep yourself safe from the monster under your bed as a child. Whatever. The circumstances will have been different, but you've tasted that fight or flight reaction, that adrenaline rush.

Now amplify those emotions to the proper level. What if that lost in the supermarket fear hadn't been resolved in just a few minutes? What if you'd had to find your own place to sleep that night? What if you hadn't been able to stop running? Would your legs have given out? Were your other senses dulled or sharpened? Imagine all your attention on the threat pursuing you until the pain in your body explodes into your consciousness? What would it feel like to have all the pain of running too far hit you all at once?

All those experiences are going to help you connect with your characters in new ways. Take note of your body's response to the memory as well. Are your shoulders tense? What expression are you wearing? How do others perceive your face when the memory is full upon you? There are lots of ways to explore this in ways that add color and authenticity for readers.

Measure The Stakes

In addition to emotional memory, when ratcheting up your own emotions to the appropriate levels, measure the stakes for your character. What do they want (and stand to lose)? How do they plan to achieve that goal? What experience have you had that is close to that?

Let's walk through a potential scene. Tina is a teenage girl who is pregnant (unplanned) and now has to tell her parents.

Tina has to confess to something she knows will disappoint her parents. Ever had to confess to something you knew would hurt someone you care about? Ever made a decision that disappointed someone you cared about?

Tina's pregnant because she got drunk at a party and slept with her boyfriend without protection. Ever got caught up in the moment and then regretted it later? Ever had someone with more experience, someone who was older, lead you down the wrong path regardless of the harm it might cause you? (I might have once convinced my little brother a broken dog biscuit was a cookie...)

Tina's worked really hard to earn an athletic scholarship to university in the fall and now all of that is at risk. Ever had a situation where something you'd been planning for, a dream even, just fell apart? Ever been forced to choose between bad and worse?

Maybe you have more in common with Tina's character than you thought, right. Now, let's measure what's at stake for Tina. We have to filter the storytelling through Tina's worldview, so we have to know what her family's "rules" (spoken or unspoken) are about unplanned or unwed pregnancies.

Will she walk into this situation expecting a verbal assault or support? Does admitting she's pregnant require her to admit to other things like lying or sneaking out or underage drinking or seeing a boy her parents disapprove of? How does she feel about the pregnancy? How does she feel about the father?

All of these additional stakes will help amplify the emotions in the scene.

Now we layer in the WHY. Why is Tina facing her parents instead of running away, going to a clinic, or simply ignoring the problem for now? What is her goal in this scene? Is she looking for a confrontation or hoping for support to make a difficult decision? Is this pregnancy a way out of a future she didn't want, a road block, or imminent disaster?

By using emotional memory, you can create an intimate perspective for readers that will draw them deeper into the story. In most scenarios, there are shared experiences you can draw on even if the circumstances or intensity don't line up precisely.

Take Care Of Yourself

We've all likely read different news reports of method actors who took the preparation for their role too far. If you're exploring painful or traumatic memories, be sure to surround yourself with appropriate supports and have someone who cares about you to talk through things if needed.

My personal rule when I am writing really intense emotional scenes where I'm heavily drawing upon emotional memory is to take a day off afterwards. Once I have the first draft done of that scene, I take a day off. I break up my writing day by going for a walk, read a book. Do whatever helps you to de-stress and find some mental equilibrium.

CREATING CHARACTER VOICE

In deep POV, we should strive to ensure that each of our POVCs (and even the more prominent minor characters) have unique voices. This is not the same as author voice. The stories that you choose to tell and how you choose to tell them makes up your author voice.

There are certain unique promises we make to readers from book to book. What makes a Stephen King book a Stephen King book? Or a Nora Roberts book a Nora Roberts book? It doesn't matter which characters they create to populate their stories, there are certain storytelling promises as a reader you expect to be kept by authors from book to book. Author voice is actually more about branding.

Character voice is something different. Character voice is unique to each character and characters should be different from one book to another. Many authors have a set of twenty (plus or minus) characters they draw upon over and over: the arrogant hero, the feminist teenager, the clumsy newbie, you get the idea. But from one book to another those characters should sound different (excluding recurring characters of course).

So, how do we create unique character voice in deep POV? You need to nail this in order for readers to connect with your characters. Otherwise it ends up being akin to that person you don't know very well who's completely over-sharing about their personal problems. It gets really uncomfortable fast. If readers don't care about your POVC, hearing about their intimate thoughts and problems could have readers seeking a bookmark.

The backbone of character voice in deep POV is description, internal dialogue, and subtext.

The Author Needs To Be Invisible

In deep POV, the goal is to remove the author's voice entirely if possible. The story must read like it's coming directly from the POVC and the writer becomes invisible. Imagine the POVC and your reader share a mind. You, the writer, are not the filter for the story, but instead the filter is the POVC's own history, past experiences, opinions, motivations, priorities, prejudices, etc.

What would the character notice or comment on about their surroundings or the people they meet? What would stand out to that character? What stands out as odd, out of place, or remarkable for your character? This not only helps the reader learn what "normal" is for this character, but pulls readers into the story through your character's eyes.

Someone who's grown up in a trailer park will notice different things than someone who's grown up in a mansion. A vegan and a farmer who raises beef cattle may both be against animal cruelty and neglect, but how they express that passion will look different. Two sisters who grew up together both have a desire to become doctors to help people, but one becomes a plastic surgeon and the other takes a job with Doctors Without Borders. The sisters' priorities, preferences and experiences will influence how they take in and interpret everything they see and the people they meet because they will place value or significance on different things.

I'm a country mouse through and through. An empty dirt road or forest path with my dog by my side is my idea of adventure. Give me farm fields and open windows. When I must go to Toronto, I'm on edge and stressed. I'm in unfamiliar territory. Everything that I take in while I'm in the city, usually, is filtered through my distaste of being there. The buildings don't gleam in the sun, they loom, they're cold and intimidating. The city isn't buzzing with activity and innovation, it's exhausting—it never sleeps.

This is how you apply your POVC's filter to the story. How do they see the world? What do they want? How do they react when they can't have what they want?

Avoid the Obvious

Description can bring a scene, place, or character to life, but too much or too little can break the fictive dream for readers. A reader will do ninety percent of the work creating a mental image of a character, the setting and the fictional world, but if the writer is too sparing with description the reader can't fill in the gaps. If the story is bogged down with unnecessary description, readers begin to skim (the fictive dream is broken) or they'll just quit.

The sweet spot is to share just enough details, filtered through your POVC, to let the reader create their own image. Readers don't need a visual play-by-play of every item the character sees. They will lean in and wonder WHY the character has noticed one aspect over others. What does it say about the character? About the environment they're in?

Skim over the details that would be expected and focus on the details that stand out to your character and choose something that shows readers something about the POVC's personality, goals, or character arc. Everyone knows the sky is blue and clouds are white. Don't tell readers the woman your POVC just met has a mouth, two eyes, a nose or two ears—what's unusual? And how does what your POVC notices give the reader insight into her and this new character?

"Ender looked at Peter only to detect anger or boredom, the dangerous moods that almost always led to pain." *Ender's Game* by Orson Scott Card.

BOOM! This description not only tells us about the boy being observed, but the character doing the observing.

Readers don't want a catalog of every item in the room, they want to know how your POVC feels about specific objects in the room. What your POVC notices first, how they interpret that object's presence in the room, and how it makes them feel is character gold. Don't waste an opportunity to show readers what kind of person your POVC is by listing, cataloging, or otherwise reporting on what's going on.

Let Characters Describe Setting As They Interact With It

Avoid narrative dumps of description. This does little to help readers understand or get to know your POVC. Which details must the reader know? Avoid dropping in those details like bird poop on a car window. Let description paint a word picture, not splatter art.

Instead of cataloging how many pairs of shoes (their color or sizes) are discarded haphazardly in the front hallway of a home, have your character step over or pick their way through the mess. How do they feel about that? Is that normal and do they see this as a normal lived-in home? Is this seen as sloth-like housekeeping? Are they cringing at the realization of how many children they're about to face?

Let them sweep the discarded shoes out of their way with their foot, pause to organize and match each pair, walk over the shoes without care, or tiptoe through the mess—any of those details would tip off the reader about how the POVC feels and at the same time paints a word picture for your reader.

When you have a character interact with the setting, it provides an organic reason for the character to think about it. Thoughts seem to pop into our heads randomly, but much of the time there's a thread of connection. Something has sparked the thought. Your POVC walks into a kitchen and smells the lilacs blooming outside and that triggers a happy memory. That's fine. Let the POVC open a window and then react to the scent wafting in from outside. Let them pause over a vase of lilacs on a table and breathe in the scent. Do you see the difference?

Let's try an example.

I walked into a rectangular room with a bay window and upscale furniture in artful arrangement. A Persian rug covers the floor. A large twenty-seat dining table dominates the next room and beyond that the kitchen gleams with stainless steel everything.

This has created a very detailed word picture, fair enough, but the reader has no idea how the POVC feels about being there.

Instead, let your POVC interact with the setting and share their impression (feelings) of the room in a way that reveals character.

I stepped where Caroline stepped. With each new room she toured me through, I gathered close all the loose bits and flaps of my clothing and stayed away from the ornamented edges. If 'you break it you bought it' applies here, I'll be broke before we get to the kitchen and the promised tea.

Familiarity will influence what a POVC notices and how they feel about it. When you walk into your own house, you notice different things than someone who walks in for the first time. We might focus on the small imperfections, the dirt smudge on the door frame, that our guests don't notice. Sometimes we don't see things as they actually are, but the look of disgust on our guest's face tips us off that our house keeping is lacking.

Keep in mind that some details are noticed immediately and others take a bit more time to register. A character might not notice the chill in the air until the adrenaline rush wears off, for instance.

Precise Word Choice For Description That Has Punch

The words your character uses to describe things builds on their voice. Connotation is important to pay attention to. Some words come with baggage, a history of associations that can be negative or positive. If I have a character working in a forced labor camp, I wouldn't call it a concentration camp unless I intended for readers to associate it with the German camps in WWII.

Naked and nude are two words I like to play with. They mean more or less the same thing, but the connotation for each word implies different things. Naked implies a lack of clothing, exposure, vulnerability. Nude implies a natural state, confidence, beauty.

Some Examples

"Yes, father," Bran told him. He looked up. Wrapped in his furs and leathers, mounted on his great warhorse, his lord father loomed over him like a giant." *Game of Thrones*, George R.R. Martin

Martin emphasizes his POVC's stature (a child) as well as how the boy sees his father. Bran is impressed and intimidated by his father, yet knows he holds a privileged position. His lord father loomed. Bran could have described his father a million different ways, but Bran sees that his father casts a long shadow. Just a word and we can infer how Bran feels about his father through his description.

"But I ain't never seen a baby yell like Mae Mobley Leefolt. First day I walk in the door, there she be, red-hot and hollering with the colic, fighting the bottle like it's a rotten turnip." *The Help*, Kathryn Stockett

The baby is red-hot and hollering, that's not a normal sight for this character, but more than that the character diagnoses the problem at just a glance. The baby is fighting the bottle like it's a rotten turnip. Turnips aren't the preferred food of choice for wealthy people, typically. It's a plain and cheap vegetable, so what can we infer about the character based on the items she's familiar with she uses as comparisons?

The setting and description should mirror how the character feels. The setting and description should lend subtext (we'll get to that shortly) to a character's goals and motivations. That seems like a lot, but it's simply precise word choice and word associations.

What Forces Are At Work?

You must take into account all of the forces at work for and against your POVC in any scene and let that influence their words, their body language, their thoughts, and how they see and interact with the world around them. You shouldn't need to TELL your readers anything, they will infer how your character FEELS through description.

Let's consider this scenario:

Ed and Sarah are in love and want to make plans together for that night.

Ed and Sarah are in love and want to make plans together for that night, but Sarah is Ed's boss' daughter and if Dad finds out Ed will lose his job, so they hide their love. Ed doesn't want Sarah to think he's ashamed of her or afraid of her father, but he really needs this job. Then his boss asks him to work late.

All of these things are at play in Ed's head and heart. How would these factors color how he sees and interacts with the world? Because how he views the world at any given time will affect the way he describes settings and people.

If Ed is hopeful he can keep all the balls in the air, then that arrogance and confidence will shine through.

Ed strode into the office, the room lit with the last orange rays of the day promising a warm evening.

If he's tired and questioning whether the girl or the job is worth all the trouble, that will similarly affect the way he interprets and filters the world around him.

Ed trudged into the office and shut the door with a soft click. The boss wouldn't turn on the lights until the sun had gone completely down and the only light in the room was the glow from his calculator display.

What's Not Noticed

Sometimes, the best way to show how your character feels is not to describe it all. This sounds counter-intuitive but stay with me. Let's look at an example:

Fallon paused in front of the full-length mirror and focused on her face and hair. Looking any lower would just ruin her day and she had a lot of shopping to do.

Why is she refusing to look at the rest of herself in the mirror? What do you infer about her level of self-confidence from this? When a POVC refuses to notice or look at something, that also shows the reader about their character and motivations.

FOUNDATIONS OF INTERNAL DIALOGUE

Internal dialogue is a character's inner thoughts. Mastering this is vital because much of deep POV is the internal workings of a character's mind. In line with creating a seamless immersive experience for readers, internal dialogue is not italicized in deep POV or tagged with he/she thought.

What Internal Dialogue Is Not

Internal dialogue is not telepathy or mind speak. For those who are writing fantasy or speculative fiction, mind speak and/or telepathy can be important story elements, but don't confuse it with internal dialogue. If you're using telepathy or mind speak, use italics to set it apart from internal dialogue.

Internal dialogue is not narration. Contemporary examples of narration would be the *I Am Number Four* series by Pittacus Lore or Lemony Snicket's *A Series of Unfortunate Events*. A narrator is not limited to the knowledge held by one character and is not limited by time. The narrator may look ahead, look behind, or offer a commentary about the characters' present circumstance. There are no narrators in deep POV.

Internal Dialogue is not narrative. Your character will tell the story through their observations, feelings, and interactions with people. Inside that narrative, the internal dialogue is often where the tension and emotional depth resides. These need to blend together seamlessly for the reader. It should be clear from context which is narrative and which is internal dialogue.

Inevitably I get asked at this point whether it's OK to use third person POV for narrative and first person for internal dialogue. I've seen this done well in a couple of different genres. I have never done this because it just makes my job more difficult and I like to keep things simple. If you can't do it really well, don't do it. This is going add complexity to the writing technique so make sure you're equipped to really utilize this effectively.

Internal Dialogue In Deep POV

Thoughts are not usually analytical or organized. Thoughts are not often grammatically correct so sentence fragments are acceptable. Because thoughts can be truncated and choppy, ensure the reader can follow what's going on.

People in a conversation rarely refer to what they're talking about when the subject is mutually understood. (Violating this is referred to As You Know, Bob syndrome.) In real life, this poses a problem for law enforcement using listening devices to try and overhear a criminal admitting to a crime because both parties in the conversation know what they're talking about.

You do it?

Yeah.

Any problems?

Nothing I couldn't handle.

Did they just commit murder to take out the trash? In fiction, the internal dialogue and subtext must explain what's actually being discussed. Resist the temptation to tell or break POV to make sure readers "get it." If beta readers can't follow along or stumble to figure out what's going on, examine your internal dialogue and subtext.

Use simple subject/verb construction. Most people don't think in complete or complex sentences. We rarely use clauses and phrases or even symbolism. *I've gotta get out of here.* Spoken dialogue can be more complex if that's part of your character's make up, but for internal dialogue to feel natural keep it simple.

Internal dialogue usually elicits a physical response such as a change in posture, tone of voice, facial expression or a physical reaction like sweating or shivering. Internal dialogue can elicit a softening or a hardening outwardly. The man who picks up the phone expecting it to be his boss might have a professional or hard edge to his tone, but his voice softens when he hears his wife's voice instead.

The Internal Dialogue Web

Remember our story web? The circular layers of the web will be things like action scenes and character arc scenes. Those scenes are connected by internal dialogue making sense of each scene. A tug in one corner of the web is felt across the whole web. Internal dialogue should affect body language and tone of voice, actions, decisions, dialogue—all of it. Readers know WHY the POVC is doing any of these things because of internal dialogue. Action needs internal dialogue to explain the thought motivating that action.

Internal Dialogue Is About Filtering & Interpreting

Every POVC has a unique set of filters they view the world through. The POVC needs to interpret everything they see and hear and feel through that worldview for the reader. The POVC must not objectively report what they see or hear, but rather filter and/or interpret everything and everyone they meet in the story. Readers want to know what the character thinks and feels about things.

Where internal dialogue is too sparse, deep point of view can leave readers confused and frustrated. There are just strings of actions and reactions and the reader is left wondering why any of this is going on and how it's all connected. If your beta readers are struggling to connect, one issue to check is whether there's enough internal dialogue providing (not explaining) evidence for the WHY. If the POVC knows something the reader knows it, but that's all the reader knows.

Basic Deep Point of Rules Apply To Internal Dialogue

The same rules of limiting distance, avoid naming emotions and senses, creating immediacy—these still apply in internal dialogue. Examine your own thoughts for a moment. Have you ever said to yourself: I'm mad/sad/depressed/frustrated. Probably not. You'll rant or rehearse arguments you should've said. You'll blame yourself and self-flagellate with negative thoughts. You'll avoid thinking about the obvious right-in-front-of-you truth.

Some people are very thought (if that isn't a word it is now). Some people think things to death. They prepare or rehearse in their heads, they talk to themselves all the way through, and then examine everything to the minutest degree in hindsight. However, it's likely more common that in times of stress and conflict (especially when the fight, flight or freeze response is triggered) that our thoughts become sparser. We're still thinking things, but how we talk to ourselves changes given the circumstances and the time allowed between the stimuli and the response.

How Personality Plays Into Internal Dialogue

How self-aware is your character of their emotions and hang ups? How intent is your character on numbing, avoiding, or distracting themselves from discomfort? Do they regain control by taking charge or by taking the blame? Some personalities are more self-aware and introspective than others.

James Scott Bell in his book *Write Your Novel From The Middle,* teaches about the self-reflection that happens in the center of a story where the POVC realizes something about themselves. Either they recognize a flaw they need to shore up, give up on something they had previously wanted, realize a truth about themselves and decide to change at any cost. That shift in awareness, the necessity to become self-aware, can create a compelling emotional arc for your story and often you show that through internal dialogue.

Building Tension Into Internal Dialogue

Internal dialogue can shine a spotlight on the disparity between a character's comfort zones and their reality. Comfort zones are the situations, places, people, and events a character is familiar with and knows how to navigate without much stress. The problem with comfort zones is there's no tension or conflict there. Story is created when a character is faced with external (and/or internal) pressure that conflicts with what they want, know, believe to be normal, or consider to be possible.

Internal dialogue can tip off the reader that the POVC knows they're embarking on a lost cause or highlight that they're aware of the right (or wrong) thing despite how it affects their current goals or plans.

Let's look at two movies that offered a similar scenario and see how internal dialogue helped and plagued each character.

- Tom Hank's movie *Sully* was about a pilot who saved all lives aboard the plane after a catastrophic mechanical failure.
- Denzel Washington's movie *Flight* was about a pilot who saved all lives aboard the plane after a catastrophic mechanical failure.

Sully, Tom Hank's character, was more self-aware and confident. His internal dialogue propped him up despite the handicap of Acute Stress Disorder (the short-lived cousin on PTSD). Though he had doubts and faced incredible external pressure, he knew he had done everything right. He had his down moments, but he knew what he knew and he stood up to the bully.

Denzel Washington's character was only able to save everyone because he was drunk and when he was faced with external pressure his internal dialogue (through a lens of addiction) became his worst enemy. We saw the destructive power of poor thinking and a lack of self-awareness. He was an expert at rationalizing everything, but the truth kept sneaking back in and causing him problems. He was at war with himself, but he just wasn't interested in winning the war.

Your character's internal dialogue can push them to keep going or convince them to quit. Many runners say that once you tell yourself you're in pain, once you begin to question whether you can make it in your head, you'll quit. When all things are equal, running is as much a mental game as it is a physical one.

Will your POVC's internal dialogue help them through tough times or be the reason they can't get out of the trough? Make sure to link all the action and forward momentum together with internal dialogue (remember the web) so the reader understands the WHY and continues cheering for the POVC.

SUBTEXT: THE ELEPHANT IN THE ROOM

Subtext relates to the unspoken communication between characters. Non-verbal communication can include gestures, voice tone and volume, facial expressions (including micro expressions which flash across a face for the barest of moments), physiology (sweating, blushing) and posture. These all combine to create what *Psychology Today* called a silent orchestra that makes up communication. Studying body language, and how non-verbal communication can influence perception and behavior is vital to writing in deep POV.

Adult conversations often have many layers of meaning that might not have much to do with what's actually said. Euphemisms or code words stand in for topics or people both adults are familiar with. The key is to make sure the reader is aware of the unspoken conversation going on and this is often done through body language and internal dialogue.

Take the example below of a mother speaking with her teenage son the morning after he's missed his curfew:

Mom: Came in pretty late last night.

Son: Yep.

Mom: You promised it wouldn't happen again.

Son: I know.

Without internal dialogue and some beats, we don't really know what the subtext of this conversation is. Did the son miss curfew because he pulled an all-nighter at the library studying and mom is just concerned about his health? Is the son frequently abusive and this conversation is more of a power struggle, an and-what-are-you-gonna-do-about-it conversation? There's plenty of room here for subtext and additional layers of meaning for readers.

Familiarity Changes Subtext

The more time people spend together, the subtler their communication becomes. When one person has a lot to lose, the conversation often includes built-in deniability with ambiguities and double speak. Let's look at an example. A couple is repairing their marriage after the husband admits to an affair and he's late coming home.

Wife: *Working late again?* (Where were you really? Who were you with?)

Husband: *Yeah, there's a big client meeting in the morning. Steve was there too. I stopped and bought you flowers.* (I really was working late. I thought about you. Please believe me.)

The wife can respond to the unspoken question in several ways without blatantly revealing how she perceives his behavior.

She could bury her nose in the blooms but watch his face for any sign that he's lying. (I want to trust you, but I'm not sure I trust myself.)

Accept the flowers. "They're lovely. Thank you." (I'm choosing to trust you.)

Leave him holding the flowers. "There's a plate for you in the fridge. I'm going to bed." (I'm not saying you're lying, but I just can't give you the benefit of the doubt.)

When one person is unwilling to bring up what they're really talking about, it could be a reflection of an inequal balance of power, a lack of trust, a lack of privacy, or dislike of conflict.

Subtext Requires Interpretation For Readers

Interpretation is very important. Your POVC has to decide what the body language means or reveal what they're trying to communicate through body language so readers can follow along. Subtext will fall flat if the reader doesn't understand there's another level of meaning happening, so make sure your POVC gives enough evidence to communicate how they're feeling, or let the reader know the POVC is guessing at what the deeper level of meaning is. Give the reader enough evidence to decide if the POVC's interpretation is trustworthy or not.

Many women will smile to cover discomfort. This is often misinterpreted by aggressive men who see the smile as playing hard to get and press harder. Do the women really send mixed messages with body language, or are aggressive men blind to body language? Subtext requires interpretation. What does your character perceive is being said? What cues (body language) led them to that conclusion? If it's the wrong conclusion, make sure to leave a couple of breadcrumbs for the reader to know the POVC is being duped.

Relationships and Intimacy and Subtext

Intimacy allows us to make unspoken demands on another's time or actions. The more two characters share (history, past experiences, social standing, culture) the subtler the subtext can become. This is a great way to show the depth or complexity of a relationship through showing and not telling and avoid those awkward info dumps editors gleefully cross out.

In order for your POVC to make these leaps and assumptions about how others feel or what they're communicating (aside from universal gestures such as tapping a watch when they want to leave), it's important to show readers this relationship or familiarity, but you must use a little art.

What do I mean by that? Early on, build in the ability for two characters to read each other. It doesn't have to be long, nor do the insights gained need to be significant. Consider the wife sitting down to have tea with her husband and prepares his drink just the way he likes it, different from hers, without request or instruction. The specificity with which she makes his tea shows readers the familiarity they share.

What about the boy who doesn't like the way another guy is looking at his girl at a party? He could blow up and cause a scene, or more likely he'd let the other guy know to back off without using any words. A hand at her waist, a kiss on the cheek while staring at the other guy would both be effective.

What about the girl who notices the other guy's attention? Does she smile and keep meeting his glance, or does she touch the guy she's with, lean into her boyfriend or maybe or grab his hand? Question asked and answered without a word.

How much information is conveyed through body language will depend on the depth and length and intensity of the characters' relationships. The couple who has just begun dating is going to struggle interpreting body language more than the couple who's been married for fifty years. Teenage girls seem to have subtext mastered, the entire group can break out in a fit of giggles over an eye roll.

Let's go deeper.

Laurel straightened the shoes and school bags strewn haphazardly around the entry way. Three bags packed for a weekend. Never had to remind the kids it was their weekend with their Dad. She put the kettle on the stove to boil and pulled out two mugs.

Laurel leaned one hip against the counter and tucked her hair behind her ears. She stared at the clock on the wall. The second hand ticked with searing finality. The kettle whistled and she dropped a teabag in each mug and poured in the hot water. The archaic rumble of a Hemi engine pulled in the drive. The driver's door slammed shut and Paul's signature three-knuckled rap sounded on the front door. She didn't leave the counter.

"Laurel? Are the kids ready?"

No more delaying. "In here."

The screen door screeched open and banged shut. His steel-toed boots scuffed across her clean floor and paused at the door to the kitchen. "Hey. Sorry I'm late. Are the kids ready?"

She turned to face him. She didn't hide the droop in her shoulders or put on a fake smile.

He stared at her a moment longer than normal. "You OK?"

"Can we talk for a minute?" She held up the two mugs of hot water and nodded towards the table.

"Sure." He sat, his legs stretched out to the side. He still wore his blue work uniform and he hadn't loosened the laces on his boots yet. "What's up?"

She set the mugs in front of him and went back for the sugar, honey, and milk. Her grandmother would be appalled that they were using mugs and not teacups. Paul dropped two teabags into the water. He left the ordinary tea bag to steep and dipped the herbal tea bag up and down three times in the other mug before he lifted the tea bag out and slid the herbal tea across the table to her.

She drizzled a bit of honey in her mug and stirred. The spoon rattled off the sides. After a minute of silence, Paul lifted the tea bag out of his mug and Laurel slid the sugar and milk closer to him.

She tapped the side of her mug with a chipped-polish fingernail. Just blurt it out. "I lost my job."

He used her spoon to measure two overflowing spoonfuls of sugar into his mug and stirred it in. "Couple of weeks ago. I heard." He poured in just enough milk to give the tea a creamy look.

"You heard?" She studied his face. There was no judgment or condescension there, just the usual lines made deeper by fatigue. "You never said anything."

"Kids told me." Paul took a tentative sip to test the temperature and met her gaze over the rim of the mug. "Figured you'd tell me eventually." His mouth pulled to the side like it did when he was beating himself up for something. "Or not."

How does the subtext hint at their relationship? With just

small details, readers can figure out they've been married long enough to have three children but are now separated. They have a routine for making tea together, they know exactly how each other likes it. They share a sugar spoon. She's watching his body language close for hints of his thoughts, she knows what to look for. There's a history of hurt and confusion there, and maybe some regret on his part. There's not a lot of dialogue, but quite a lot has been said.

Not every bit of subtext needs to be explained with internal dialogue. Some gestures and body language are fairly universal so trust your readers to figure it out. Not all subtext is intended to be subtle.

Matt shut the hatchback and pulled his keys from his pocket giving them a good shake. Sarah glanced at him and smiled but continued talking to the woman loading groceries into the car parked next to them. They'd bought the same dog food.

He opened the driver's side door and rested an elbow on the roof. Sarah didn't look back at him. He cleared his throat. She turned to look at him and he owled his eyes. It was time to go. She didn't even know this woman.

Sarah rolled her eyes. She took a card from the other woman. Exchanging phone numbers or some such. Matt slumped into the driver's seat and turned the engine.

Sarah slid into her seat a moment later and put on her seatbelt without looking at him. "That was rude."

There were a lot of universal gestures here that wouldn't need internal dialogue to explain. Where internal dialogue is needed is providing evidence about the WHY here: what emotion Matt is feeling and what's causing that emotion?

Writing Subtext Of Other Characters

How do you stay only in your POVC's head in any scene, but also make sure the reader gets the information they need about other characters? Your POVC is able to observe other characters (are they blushing, bouncing their knee every time they try and sit still, keep glancing at the clock on the wall), evaluate what their body language is really saying, and interpret what the other character says. Let's look at some common scenarios and workarounds to avoid breaking POV.

Shane knew Sara was lying.

Shane is the POVC in this line. How does Shane know Sara is lying? Unless he actually does know, this is a POV break. Where subtext comes into this is presenting evidence to the reader to show the POVC has a reason for this assumption. She was lying, her fingers were crossed behind her back. Something like that. Make sure the reader understands why or how your POVC came to that conclusion (it doesn't have to be a long explanation).

Dan focused on picking the lock, unfazed by the child screaming behind the closed door.

If Dan isn't the POVC, then how would the POVC know Dan was fazed or unfazed. The POVC can only interpret what they see. Dan could seem unfazed, he can appear calm, but the POVC can't know what's going on in Dan's head. With subtext, you can leverage whatever relationship Dan and the POVC have to show readers a deeper insight, but you still have to give a reason for this leap in assumptions.

Dan went back to work on the lock as if the screams from the other side of the door weren't loud enough to be heard by neighbors.

This qualifier tips off the reader that the POVC is guessing, making an educated guess, about how Dan feels. K.M. Weiland calls subtext the black belt of fiction writing. It's tricky to learn, but once you get the hang of it, subtext will deepen your writing in new ways and really draw readers into your story.

INCORPORATING ALL THE SENSES

Incorporating all the senses is a piece of advice echoed on every blog for beginning writers, it seems. However, when writing in deep POV the senses are another gateway into character voice and reveal emotional arc.

We take in our surroundings through all five senses, and sometimes even that hard-to-define sixth sense as well. Different senses are associated strongly with specific things. As was touched on in the chapter on internal dialogue, it's important for thoughts and actions to have a cause. Random thoughts seem to pop into our heads, but often there's a trigger. Something we've seen, heard, felt, smelled triggered the association with that thought.

Writers are usually very good at writing sight and the other senses can be forgotten or at least not used to their full potential. We want to provide readers with an immersive fictive dream and we take in information with all of our senses every day. Senses are a great way to organically create a scenario for the POVC to have a thought precisely when you need them to.

Smell and taste are often directly correlated to memory. The scent of baking cinnamon rolls reminds me of Grandma's kitchen. We make decisions and choose a course of action based on what we see, often, which is why this is the dominant sense in life and fiction. A guy sees a pretty girl, that causes a thought that leads to an action.

Sound often evokes an emotional reaction. Think about the sound of fingers down a chalkboard, coyotes howling at night, or wooden shutters banging in the wind. My daughter tore the ligaments in her ankle doing flips on the trampoline and I happened to catch the injury on video. There was an audible crack before she screamed out in pain.

We told the doctors and nurses in the ER what had happened and they were professional but not overly sympathetic. When I showed them the video and they heard the crack (we were sure she'd broken her ankle), they all visibly cringed. The nurse made the intern watch, the intern made the doctor watch, the doctor checked the x-ray again and asked another doctor for a second opinion. They were as sure as we were that the ankle was broken. (Apparently, a ligament audibly cracking when it tears is something they'd read about in textbooks but never encountered themselves.) The sound caused an emotional response.

These senses are a gateway to ratcheting up a POVC's response in any given scene. Let's dive deeper.

What's The Most Prominent Sense?

It would be overwhelming to incorporate every sense in a scene. Instead, choose the most prominent detail to that character. Which sense in any scene will best show insight into your character based on their fears, past experiences and associations, level of tension, etc. You must be strategic in choosing which sensory details to bring out or enhance so that you can provide evidence to the reader about what's important to the POVC, what their priorities are, what they'll compromise on or be passionate about.

The Pine Tree

Let's say your POVC is climbing a pine tree. What sensory details would stand out to them? Choose the sensory details that will also show the reader insights into your POVC. They may notice the smell of the needles and associate that smell with a specific memory—negative or positive. Perhaps the most prominent sense in this situation is the sap stuck to their palms because they're neat freaks and hate getting their hands dirty.

What if they rip their shirt or their jeans? For a perfectionist or someone very concerned about their appearance or looking good, damaging clothing or getting twigs and needles in their hair could be very distressing. Maybe they're afraid of heights so they notice the way the tree sways and the branches creak with the wind. What aspect of their personality would trigger a sensitivity to a particular sense, or make them focus on a particular sense? The perfectionist might not be overwhelmed by the smell or be scared by the height or movement of the tree, but lose their mind over a tiny tear in their Canada Goose winter jacket.

Touch and Subtext

Touch is one sense that many writers use effectively, but if you combine touch with subtext you'll take your writing to the next level. What else is the touch communicating both to the POVC and other characters? That brush on the arm could be innocent or an attempt at flirtation. The silent orchestra in addition to the POVC's internal dialogue will provide evidence you can show the reader to help reveal the subtext.

Some touches are benign and socially acceptable: a handshake, a kiss on the cheek in greeting, an inadvertent brush as you pass another, being squeezed in a crowded space (like an elevator). A touch that isn't wanted is interpreted differently and could trigger all sorts of feelings depending on the context.

At the same time, nearness or touching can lend comfort. Think of the child recently injured who needs a kiss to make them feel better. The woman who leans into her man's side when she's feeling threatened. The soldier recently returned from a theater of war hugs and kisses his wife. Don't be afraid to layer in subtext as well. What else could the touch communicate and how might it be answered.

As powerful as touching is, almost touching can convey many things too. The hand raised to cup a cheek that falls away without touching could communicate desire that's denied, regret, farewell. Think about the boss who stands a little too close to his female secretary, is he being protective, authoritative, or flirting? The denial of touch also communicates many things depending on the context and subtext in a scene. Play around with this.

Power and Authority With Touch Adds Subtext

In cases of sexual harassment and abuse, power imbalances are closely looked at because the person in power doesn't need to use force or physical threats in order to command compliance. The boss who could get a woman fired doesn't have to threaten physical violence to coerce her into doing something she doesn't want to. He might not even have to blatantly state what he wants from her.

How might that subtext play out? Crowding her personal space. A finger trailing down her arm, a hug that lasts a moment too long, a hand on the small of her back guiding her into a room she doesn't want to go to. Remember to provide evidence of how the character feels about this through internal dialogue and body language.

Arun touched the gold earrings he'd given her the day their daughter was born and captured his gaze with her own. "She needs a name."

He cupped Arun's cheek in his palm. "Then give her one. She is old enough."

Arun lowered her gaze and turned her face away from his touch.

Kaduis sighed. "I cannot. At least not publicly."

Did you catch the power imbalance above? No direct question is asked, but there's an underlying question (touching the earrings) and it's the question asked through subtext that's answered. Will you publicly name the child and acknowledge she's yours?

His touch is more about asserting authority than affection and she rejects that dominance by withdrawing from his touch. His reaction to the rejection tells us much about who he is and how he treats women. Another man might have further invaded her space or simply walked away as a dismissal.

So much can be implied with eye contact and touch, the withdrawal of it, and whether it's wanted or not.

TAGS VS BEATS VS STAGE DIRECTIONS

In deep POV, because we are striving for that immersive fictive dream we want to remove as much distance as possible between the reader and the POVC. We need to write tight and be economical with our words because deep POV often expands our word count. To that end, making better use of speech attribution is one easy way to have our words pull double or triple duty.

A tag is the he/she said speech attribution. This is the most unobtrusive tag and is the one most often used and recommended because readers are trained to almost not see this tag. (If you're using tags like shouted, exclaimed, proclaimed, etc. to attribute speech, that's telling.) However, all the speech tag does is tell the reader who is speaking.

Instead, strive to use more beats in your novels. A beat is an action or bit of internal dialogue that attributes speech, so it pulls double duty. Beats not only show the reader who's speaking but also moves the story forward.

(Tag) "I like the purple sweater." Jennifer said. She pulled the hanger off the rack and held it up.

(Beat) Jennifer pulled the purple sweater off the rack and held it up. "I like this one."

Both of these convey the same information. By using a beat instead of a tag, we've tightened up the word count without losing any meaning. We can switch it up and put the dialogue first, but it's still clear who is speaking.

"I like this one." Jennifer pulled the purple sweater off the rack and held it up.

Many books and teachers will say when writing in deep pov there are no tags, only beats. This is true and it isn't. There are many bestselling authors who write in deep point of view (or at least a very personal and intimate point of view) who sparingly use speech tags. My personal rule is keep it tight. If you don't need the speech tag, lose it. If you find you're using stage directions simply to avoid using a tag, maybe that's an appropriate place for a tag.

Where Beats Pull Their Own Weight

Even the best dialogue can fall flat without effective beats weaving in character thoughts, feelings and/or backstory. Beats also keep the reader rooted in the setting in long back and forth dialogue scenes. Beats can help vary the pace, prevent ongoing dialogue from becoming just talking heads to our readers, attribute dialogue, and identify the POVC in any scene.

A beat can be a physical action or gesture or it could be a snippet of internal dialogue. You probably have a default gesture or action. I do. Your character might have a signature gesture or action that's a tell for an emotion, but like everything else, use it sparingly so it stands out. Otherwise it can pull the reader from the story and just become laughable.

When I go through a first draft, my characters have busy hands, they're always shoving hands in pockets or touching their hair, waving, etc. These are stage directions.

Avoid Stage Directions

Stage directions are when your character does an action or gesture that doesn't move the story ahead or show your readers anything about a POVC's desires, motivations or goals. They are simply moving from stage left to stage right.

Some common stage directions would be: reached, pushed, pulled, tipped, turned, looked, walked, entered, exited, glanced, lifted.

This is where you take your writing to the next level. Avoid stage directions and push for beats. Let's look at an example. I've bolded the stage directions that aren't moving the story ahead or revealing anything about the character speaking.

"Can I show you something?"

The man ***turned*** *and shrugged. "I had to see it one last time."*

Her mouth hung open a moment. He had owned that painting? "Mr. Silas?"

"It's just Silas." **He waved his glass at the room.** *"I love your gallery. You should advertise more."*

Catherine stared. *He had the most beautiful green eyes. She cleared her throat. "My source said your collection was in Europe." Her source had also told her the painting had been an impulse buy and was kept in storage.*

He shrugged. *"When I discovered the buyer was in Boston, I had to come and visit."*

Catherine smiled. *"Let me show you around."*

The bolded bits are stage directions rather than beats. There's very little for a reader to glean from this about either character. They are moving, you know who's speaking, but there's not much here beyond the dialogue. Further, there's some internal dialogue that's slowing down the pace. I've changed it up below to try and fix those problems.

His dark curls, more of a messed-on-purpose coif, framed his face like a broken halo. She'd bet good money he'd never thrown a hay-bale in his life. "Can I show you something?" His suit fit like it was tailored and he wore it well.

He nodded at the painting next to him. "I had to see it one last time."

Her brows shot up. "Mr. Silas?"

"It's just Silas." He seemed to wave away her formality. "I love your gallery. You should advertise more."

He had the most beautiful green eyes. She was staring. She glanced away and cleared her throat. "My source said your collection was in Europe."

"It was an impulse buy. Thought it was time to stop hoarding my collection and let others enjoy it too." He lifted a shoulder and winked. "When I discovered the buyer was in Boston, I had to come and visit."

Heat crept into her cheeks. Was he flirting? "Let me show you around."

So, what did I change?

I added a couple of lines of internal dialogue at the beginning to (hopefully) give a bit of backstory about where Catherine comes from (thrown a hay bale) and gave the readers a view of Silas filtered through Catherine's POV. It is a bit wordy but in line for this character. For another character I might edit that down because it does slow the pace.

The next beat revealed setting. Not a lot of setting details are needed. The reader knows it's an art gallery and the conversation is about a painting. Readers can picture the rest on their own because those finer points of the setting aren't important in this scene.

I changed "her mouth hung open" to "her brows shot up" even though the first one isn't incorrect per se. I just felt that "her mouth hung open" was a little too obvious and wanted a bit more subtlety given the setting and social context. It was a personal taste thing. The next beat was changed to show a bit more of his personality through her perception, he's not just a stuffy rich guy. He's surprised her.

In the line that starts with "Catherine stared" in the first version, I removed the stage direction. There was some author intrusion (why would she think about he he'd acquired the painting, there was no catalyst for that thought) so I gave a line of dialogue to the other character instead as a workaround. Coming from him it's additional info about his character organically added.

Is he flirting? I wanted to be ambiguous intentionally because Catherine isn't sure herself. I wanted the reader to see exactly what she saw and wonder if he was actually flirting or not. She's blushing, maybe she's not used to attention from guys like him. But maybe he's just personable and easy going. The reader gets to doubt along with her.

You might have made different changes, some of these are stylistic and voice choices, but I hope you can see a positive difference. Hopefully the second version drew you into the story a little bit more and gave you more insight into each character.

Beats should be intentional and strategic and stage directions kept to a minimum.

PACING: WHEN TO GO SHALLOW

Deep point of view can be intense and sometimes pulling back into a shallower point of view can create a variety of effects for readers when used intentionally. Part of writing in this style is knowing when to give your reader a place to catch their breath and when to keep them leaning in.

Action and Reaction

Every action (or thought) has an equal and opposite reaction. Action scenes are when the POVC has decided on a course of action (which may not involve any movement) and sets out on that course. Action scenes can include fights, arguments, or simply forward movement towards the story goal whatever that looks like.

Reaction scenes then are how the POVC deals with the consequences or fallout of the preceding decision. In the reaction scenes, the POVC regroups and then makes another decision which launches a new action scene. There's often internal dialogue, introspection, inaction, in a reaction scene so the pace is slowed. Be strategic about this.

This is also known as scenes and sequels if you're more familiar with that terminology. This happens more at the story arc level. Understanding this is pretty crucial to story structure. How it applies specifically to deep POV as a technique is more at the sentence level—what Dwight Swain called Motivation Reaction Units (MRUs).

Sequencing

In deep POV, because this is such a personal and intimate method of storytelling, it's important to get the correct sequence of events happening in our character's heads. Things happen so quickly in our minds we often don't realize there is a cause and effect process happening, but there's almost always an action and reaction chain of events. By putting the cart before the horse, so to speak, the reader is jerked out of the story.

Make sure that for every decision you've made the WHY clear. Sometimes this is as simple as a few short words or an action beat in a line of dialogue. Make sure the thought comes before the dialogue.

Thought then Action
Action then Reaction

She flung open the car door and jumped. She had to get away before the next stop. (wrong sequence)

She had to get away before the next stop. She flung open the car door and jumped. (proper sequence)

This basic structure is important to adhere to. Show what the character is reacting to. This won't change what you want to happen, but providing a proper order of events helps the reader stay immersed in the story.

Jake started when a fist pounded on the door. (reaction precedes the action)

A fist pounded on the apartment door. Jake started. (action then reaction)

These small things seem nitpicky, because readers will likely sort out what you mean, but when the intent is an immersive experience the goal is to avoid forcing the readers to go over a sentence two or three times to figure out what you really meant to say. The longer the reader can immerse themselves in the story world without distraction, the more attached to your characters they'll become.

There are occasions where things happen simultaneously, you can walk AND think, for instance. These need to be kept to a minimum because most of the time the reaction is based on an action or thought of some kind. Whatever software you're using to write with, almost all of them have a search and find feature. These are the red flag words I search for that tip me off to a sequencing violation: as, while, when.

Be Strategic

Something else to keep in mind when writing in deep POV is when not to use it. There are specific reasons why you might write in a shallower POV for effect. Consider a woman flying through the house doing a last-minute speed clean before company arrives. You might choose to write that scene in a more distant or shallow POV to create the effect of time flying past or show how little thought she's putting into each specific task. These shallower point of view moments need to serve a story purpose.

Technically, in deep POV there should be a play-by-play kind of narrative for each action. The POVC hears a knock at the door, crosses the room, reaches for the knob, grasps the cool brass and turns the knob... You get the idea. This slows down the action and has the reader leaning in because if you've spent this much time on the door opening there must be something important behind it.

Sometimes you just need your character to get from point A to point B, so you'd use a shallower point of view to do that. It's just efficient and helps the reader to focus on the necessary details and maintains a faster pace.

Sometimes there's opportunity to place a reaction scene in those in-between moments. Maybe your character is in a carriage traveling, walking to school, or in the car between crime scenes, and they pause to watch people on the sidewalk or notice changes in the scenery from the last time they were there. These shouldn't be long and need to serve a purpose either for story (plot) arc or emotional arc.

High Emotions

Another reason you might use a shallower point of view is when the emotions are really high. It seems counter-intuitive when writing in deep POV to use a shallower point of view for those high-tension moments, but this can show a numbing effect really well. It can help keep your writing realistic without boring readers. For instance, someone who's been seriously injured will repeat the same phrase over and over focusing on whatever hurts. They'll chant: my arm hurts, my arm hurts, my arm hurts. They may not be able to say much else in the moment because all they're aware of is the pain. Use a shallower point of view to show this without writing out pages of the same phrase.

When your whole novel is in deep POV, using a shallower POV for high emotion scenes can force the reader to lean in more. It's the change, the surprise, in the writing style that causes the tension for readers. Whether you're trying to create an out-of-body effect, numbing effect, or a mind unable to process all the data they're taking in (articulate what they're feeling), using a shallower POV can show this very effectively. This all enhances the emotional pace of your story.

Emotional Pace

In his book *The Emotional Craft of Fiction,* literary agent Donald Maass talks about a story's emotional pace. Along with your story arc (plot), what's your character's emotional arc?

How can someone who's chased by a serial killer not be changed by that? How can finding a romantic life partner not change you? And what does that change cost? What did your character have to give up? What did they have to learn the hard way? Was this change reluctant or embraced? Was the change more about avoiding, about not becoming something? That's emotional arc.

When tension builds up, when an outlook, attitude, or prejudice has to shift in order for your POVC to reach their story goal, each emotional shift puts the emotional pace into a higher gear. The emotional pace should ratchet up the tension and coincide with the story pace and conflict.

The appeal of deep POV is the emotional journey for readers. They don't want to read a story, they want to experience it. Make them laugh, cry, shake their fist at the sky.

Let's look at an example we've already seen. I've bolded the internal dialogue.

Her father's lifeless eyes stared up at the ceiling, his mouth gaped as if he'd died mid-scream. She coughed and sputtered like she'd been punched in the gut. Her hand covered her mouth and she dropped to her knees. Crawling the short distance, she reached for the box and then withdrew her fingers. There was no mistaking Wyne's features. But that wasn't her father anymore. Her fingers trembled and tears blurred her vision. She shut the box. ***How had this happened?***

In this snippet, there's only one bare bit of internal dialogue. I wanted to give the sense that she's overwhelmed, sensory overload. She hasn't taken a moment to process what all of this means. And what's the one question that floats to the top of the mental chaos? How had this happened?

To add more internal dialogue here would've slowed the pace. I wanted to convey a sense that she was being battered with one realization after another, each one more horrifying than the last. To keep this bit in deep POV could've worked, but I was going for a specific effect. Choosing to stay close in moments of high emotional tension, or zoom out to a more shallow point of view, are stylistic choices. First ask yourself what effect you're trying to create and then decide how shallow or deep the point of view needs to be.

SETTING AND SUBTEXT

Setting is sometimes an overlooked opportunity to convey additional meaning to readers, particularly through subtext. Your setting should either heighten, change, or reflect back how your character is feeling in deep POV. This is where some art comes into play using literary devices like personification, pathetic fallacy, metaphors, similes, and others.

Let how your POVC feels show the reader what they're seeing. One of my favorite examples of this is from the opening paragraphs of *The Hunger Games* by Suzanne Collins:

"Sitting at Prim's knees, guarding her, is the world's ugliest cat. Mashed-in nose, half of one ear missing, eyes the color of rotting squash. Prim named him Buttercup, insisting his muddy yellow coat matched the bright flower. He hated me."

Katniss shows us what the cat looks like by sharing how she feels about it. Her sister has named the cat Buttercup, but Katniss describes the cat as being the color of rotting squash. How do you think Katniss feels about that cat? Collins hasn't given any backstory or info dumps, but we know not only how Katniss feels about that cat, but how she sees the world and how her sister sees the world. There's a whole lot going on in two or three short sentences describing a cat. This is economical writing.

Subtext In Setting

The objects a character surrounds themselves with can be a level of subtext. What does it say about a character who has a wall of photos, but the frames are all filled with the model photos as sold in the stores? That communicates something, right. A wall of photos of a person they're attracted to but have never spoken to? What does that say? The businessman who owns a huge executive home but has no furnishings. The drug dealer driving a $75,000 car won't pay for his son's school field trip. Do you see what I mean?

I think the original *Shrek* movie did a fabulous job of this. Audiences learned quite a lot about Lord Farquaad just from the things he surrounded himself with. Lord Farquaad's "little man" syndrome is pronounced to the point of comedy, but these are things to consider.

Use Setting To Mirror How A Character Feels

By using devices like personification, pathetic fallacy, and others you can infuse the setting and description with feelings. By giving the natural world and inanimate objects feelings and human behavior, readers can infer how the character feels. Let's look at some examples.

"Nothing says hell has to be fire, thought Ralph Truitt, standing in his sober clothes on the platform of the tiny train station in the froze middle of frozen nowhere. Hell could be like this. It could be darker every minute. It could be cold enough to sear the skin from your bones." *A Reliable Wife*, Robert Goolrick

Standing on the train platform in the frozen middle of frozen nowhere. How does Ralph Truitt feel about where he lives? About having to wait on the train platform? Does it matter what the train platform looks like? No. Most of us can picture a tiny frozen train platform.

"He bought a ticket for the first bus out, no matter where it was going. Which turned out to be an end-of-the-line place way north and west, on the shore of Lake Superior. Fundamentally the wrong direction. Colder, not warmer. But rules were rules, so he climbed aboard. He sat and watched out the window. Wisconsin flashed by, it's hayfields baled and stubbly, it's pastures worn, its trees dark and heavy. It was the end of summer." *The Midnight Line*, Lee Child

How does Jack Reacher describe Wisconsin in fall? Not terribly flattering is it. It's actually quite beautiful there in fall, but Reacher is headed somewhere he doesn't want to be, alone-again, leaving town after a relationship has ended. Do you see that how Reacher FEELS colors everything he sees? He's going to an "end-of-the-line place" that's "colder, not warmer" where the pastures look worn and the trees dark and heavy.

He doesn't see the bounty of harvest, the colored leaves, or the sunsets over pastures. He doesn't sigh with relief at the cooler temperatures or welcome the approach of fall. The way Reacher describes the setting mirrors how he feels and allows readers to infer his mood, feelings, and current outlook through subtext.

Allowing the natural world to stand in for how a character feels can be powerful, and easily inserted into a scene to add depth.

The leaves waved their encouragement. (This character is confident.)

The wind threw leaves and twigs at him, pushing against his every step forward. (This guy feels like the world is against him.)

Setting As Character

Sometimes even the setting becomes a character. A place is spoken of like it's a real person can convey a lot of things including patriotism and self-identity. Consider a work like *Outlander* by Diana Gabaldon. Scotland is almost a separate character in the first two novels in the perspective of the highlanders:

"...but make no mistake, lass, I love Scotland more, and I would give everything ... everything I have or ever will have, including my life, to see a Stuart back on the throne." Dougal McKenzie, *Outlander,* Diana Gabaldon

A Few Well-Chosen Details

Readers want to engage, to crawl into the story, and if you describe a setting down to the last cobweb, you've left the reader nothing to imagine for themselves. If I tell you my POVC has invited a guest upstairs to her bedroom, is wearing lingerie, and then shuts the bedroom door, do you need me to describe the bed, say whether there's a window or if the floor is hardwood or carpeted to create a mental image of the room?

Remember, the more time you spend describing an item or piece of the setting, the more importance the reader assumes it has. Is that item important to the story or is there an organic reason for the POVC to notice it? If you need an organic reason for a character to notice a piece of setting, have them interact with it. Don't have them catalog the solid oak coffee table, have them bump into it as they cross the room.

BACKSTORY: THE CHARACTER FILTER

Every character has a history that influences everything they say (or don't say) or do (or don't do). How you communicate this history to readers can make or break your story. Backstory is more important for you than the reader.

Internal dialogue can be used to deliver bits of backstory but it must be closely related to what's going on. If there isn't a natural trigger for the thought, it can undermine the tension or feel like an info dump/author intrusion. Remember, with backstory you answer one question and leave the reader with two more. It's a snapshot of a memory. The memory must always move the story forward, and if possible give an insight into the character at the same time.

Flashbacks are really tricky. If there's a traumatic event from a character's past you need readers to know about, instead of having the character relive the episode, show the coping mechanisms used to control the symptoms or turn their mind off. Show symptoms of anxiety (can't sit still, can't sleep, jumpy, sweating, hands trembling) and then send them for another lap around the block even though they've already done five more than usual.

With a traumatic backstory, the character will proactively seek a way to get control, but they will avoid thinking about the WHY. One effective tactic is to show the emotional arc through the slow removal of their coping mechanisms.

Netflix's *Jessica Jones* is about a girl with superhuman strength and because of a traumatic past she struggles with what seems like PTSD symptoms. Jessica has no interest in facing her past or overcoming the symptoms that take control of her life. Instead, she drinks to numb the pain, dull her emotions, and forget. You'd think this would be a hard character to cheer for, but every episode Jessica is faced with another crisis that only she can solve. She puts the bottle aside and faces her demons in order to help someone else.

But between action scenes, her first reaction is to reach for the bottle. We're never told she's struggling, the bottle is a stand in for the emotions she doesn't want/know how to deal with.

Writing Backstory

Writing backstory in deep POV isn't all that different from writing backstory in any other point of view. There are a few guidelines to help keep the pace moving and not bog down the story in extraneous details.

Backstory needs to be dripped in a drop at a time. Only give the reader what they absolutely must know in order to keep the story moving while understanding the POVC's motivations and desires.

One of the pitfalls of including backstory is that it has a tendency to strip away the suspense in a story. Use backstory to answer one reader question, but then leave them with two more.

She reached her hand through the crack in the door. The whole house was dark. Just like last time. She flipped on the light, the tightness in her shoulders easing.

This is cliché, but do you see what I mean? Don't give the reader ALL the information they need, just give them enough to keep leaning in.

Is Backstory Necessary?

As writers, our stories are a bit like icebergs. What readers see is only the part of the iceberg that's above water. Two-thirds of the iceberg is actually below the surface. You need to know so much more than the reader does. Ask yourself how much backstory the reader really needs to understand the story and how much have you included just to show you've thought of it.

Backstory Must Be Added Organically

Every bit of backstory must be organic to the story or it's author intrusion. If there's backstory the reader needs, you must create a scenario where the character would organically think of that past event.

If the reader needs information about another character, but that character isn't the POVC, then think how can the POVC give that info to the reader organically? Do they have some shared past together to draw upon? Is there body language that might hint there's more going on than what's being said? Can the POVC observe two people talking, filtering their body language, so the reader gets the information?

Felora leaned against a corner post with her back to the street, cleaning her fingernails with a small blade. Edric repressed a smile.

Even as a child, she'd hated getting her hands dirty but never had enough sense to stay out of the mud.

In this example, this is the first time readers meet my character Felora. I needed readers to understand that Edric and Felora had known each other a long time and that Edric thought her impulsive and rash. That he looked down on her. Why does he look down on her? Readers find that out later. This is pure backstory, but it doesn't read like it. It's all filtered through the POVC. Drip drip drip.

How can you use the setting to spark a memory organically? A turn of phrase? The sight of someone/something they haven't seen in a while? Smell and taste are closely linked with memory, incorporating either of those senses is an organic path to bringing up backstory.

Keep it short. Keep it totally relevant. Remember to filter it through the POVC even if it's about another character.

TIPS & TRICKS

Author Intrusion

In deep POV, the goal is to remove the author voice entirely if possible. The story must read like it's coming directly from the POVC and the writer becomes invisible. Telling is one way the author's voice intrudes into the story and creates distance for the reader. There are a few other ways that can be very subtle.

Here are a few examples: (Tavia is the POVC)

When the meal ended, Kenelm clapped. The sound bounced off the walls and the table quieted. ***Most lords employed traveling gleemen to entertain at important feasts, but Kenelm had his own scop. Tavia preferred gleemen because they recited well known songs and stories, whereas the scop composed original songs that could be quite coarse and lewd.*** *The scop approached Kenelm's chair and they spoke quietly for a moment. The scop glanced at her for a moment too long.*

The bolded bits are where my author voice intruded into the story. Why would Tavia think to herself that she preferred gleemen over scops? If she already knows the distinction, this bit of internal dialogue becomes an info dump. It breaks POV. See below for how I fixed that.

A man sat off by the fire with a lyre in his hands. He didn't wear the clothes of a nobleman, but he didn't look poor either. She poked Fin and nodded towards the man. "Who's that?"

"Kenelm's scop." Fin tipped his cup to his lips.

"A scop?" She poked him again when he didn't answer fast enough.

"Most lords employ traveling gleeman who recite well known songs and stories. Scops compose their own songs."

Something in his tone set her on edge. "Is that bad?"

"Not bad." Fin looked at her and he tipped his head towards her. "But unpredictable and often lewd."

The scop approached Kenelm's chair and they spoke. The scop glanced at her for a moment too long.

"What's he planning?" She rested her chin on the top of Fin's shoulder.

Fin gave a slight shrug. He didn't know either.

This version is much longer, but doesn't break POV. I've taken myself out of the story and instead revealed an important detail to readers in a way that's organic or natural for the character telling the story in this scene.

Here's another example:

"Can't sleep." Aralyn yawned. "I don't like this place."

The Black Forest was known for its gnarled trees, bogs, and unpredictable pits. *"It's not a nice place." Edric couldn't suppress the body shiver that rattled his spine.*

"I can feel eyes on me. Like I'm being watched."

"You are being watched." Edric widened his eyes and leaned in closer.

My editor called me on this one. This is just flat out author intrusion masquerading as narrative. The POVC wouldn't think this. Here's how I fixed it without adding many additional words:

"Can't sleep." Aralyn yawned. "I don't like this place."

"What, you don't like gnarled trees, stinking bogs, and unpredictable pits? What's wrong with you?" Edric couldn't suppress the body shiver that rattled his spine.

"I can feel eyes on me. Like I'm being watched."

"You are being watched." Edric widened his eyes and leaned in closer.

Author intrusion is sneaky and can slip in so easily. Here's a few more common ways we explain away author intrusion in deep POV that we need to watch for and eliminate.

Unbeknownst to Sarah, a monster lurked in the woods behind her house.

If Sarah doesn't know it, the reader can't either.

Jane's face went scarlet. Had she really just said that out loud?

Jane can't see her own face so how does she know it's scarlet? She could feel her face flush or heat up, but she can't see the color of her own face. This goes for the POVC describing any of their own features. I could have said, Jane combed her curly brown hair. Would Jane really think that? No. It's author intrusion. If that's information the reader needs, you have to deliver it some other way.

Ryan couldn't take his eyes off her in that Stella McCartney gown.

Unless Ryan is a fashion editor or photographer, it's unlikely that the reason he can't take his eyes of this girl is because of the label on her dress. This is author intrusion. This example works for anything a character labels: car parts, names of flowers or trees, etc. It would be natural for a mechanic to open the hood of a vehicle and know the names of the parts there, but if your character is an accountant who's never gotten grease on his hands that's author intrusion.

Sam is a bright little boy, but as you know, we've already had issues with his behavior in class."

This is "as-you-know-Bob" syndrome, but this can slip into your writing even without the 'as you know' red flag. If the POVC has a shared history or knowledge with someone, it's unlikely they would recap the past for each other. Watch for any place where characters label whatever they're talking about if both parties know the subject in question. This is where subtext and internal dialogue fill in the gaps for readers.

The Watson trope is one often used to get around giving the reader information that otherwise wouldn't be thought of by the POVC. Remember Dr. Watson from Sherlock Holmes? Watson stood in for readers and asked the questions that Holmes would never think to explain. Sometimes that's necessary. Think of any movie or book where the expert is paired with a rookie, a newbie, or someone unfamiliar with a prominent story area of expertise. It's then natural and organic for the Watson character to ask the questions the readers have without breaking POV.

The Exception

Historicals, fantasies, science fiction, these are all examples of genres that routinely incorporate terms and objects that readers might not be familiar with. Often readers will forgive a small bit of author intrusion once (at the first mention) if it's explanatory of something that's important.

Felora slid her seax, a long fighting knife, into its sheath at her hip.

But if there's a way to give that foreign object or term meaning through context, do that instead.

Felora flicked the edge of the seax with her thumb. Still sharp. She slid the knife into the sheath at her hip.

Write Tight

Writing in deep POV will/should increase your word count, but don't let your prose get lazy. Every word must not only pull its own weight, but as much as possible pull double duty. Often, writers (by my own observation) seem to fall into one of two categories with a first draft. Either the narrative is too sparse and readers can't picture what's going on, or there's a lot of extraneous verbiage that clouds and confuscates the story beyond a reader's ability to discern... you get the idea. Let's dive in a little deeper.

Redundancies

Look for any words you can remove without changing the meaning of the sentence. These are sneaky words and phrases that slip in without us even noticing. They can create subtle distance by slowing the pace and jerking the reader from the story. Sometimes redundancies are there purposely for repetition, emphasis, or character voice, and can be used with great effect (see below), but if these words and phrases are not there to serve a story purpose they need to be tightened up.

She climbed ~~up~~ the tree.

He walked across the room and ~~then~~ opened the door.

I'm a straight forward ~~and to the point~~ kind of guy.

"You is kind. You is smart. You is important." Kathryn Stockett, *The Help*

Writing On The Nose or Purple Prose

Avoid falling into purple prose. Purple prose is longer passages of pure description or narrative that don't move the story ahead. Objectively ask yourself if you need that long flowing prose about the field of lavender outside your POVC's window. If that field of lavender doesn't move the story ahead in some way or isn't integral to the plot, it may have to be scaled back or removed.

Writing on the nose is a blow-by-blow-account of something in precise detail that's unnecessary. This is where a shallower POV is helpful, you can just summarize what's going on. Instead of chronicling your POVC's journey across town, they can just catch a cab and check their watch. They're ten minutes late.

Describing in precise detail every item, bird, desk, cloud formation or walk to open the door will frustrate the reader when they realize there's no rhyme or reason for it. It's OK for your character to just brush their teeth, go to work, go to school, open a door, or drive across town.

Are There Exceptions?

Of course there are exceptions. You have to know the rules before you can break them, though. You can justify the rules you break a million different ways because some other writer who wrote a bestseller did it. Just because you can break the rules, doesn't mean you should. Be very objective and honest with yourself before breaking a rule.

Sometimes, you might write on-the-nose for a specific effect. Consider this passage:

The shot thundered across the beach, an echo of the waves. The lead bullet broke his bottom right incisor, tore through his palate, just above his upper teeth, punched through the lower bone of his eye socket, and broke through the skin just in front of his left ear. He staggered back, then dropped down into a sitting position. Pain shot through his head. The blood dripped warmly down his cheek. His left eye wouldn't focus. But he was alive. Deon Meyer, *Dead Before Dying*

This is a stylistic choice. There isn't a right or wrong amount of internal dialogue or description as long as what you keep maintains the pace you want, reveals character, and pushes the emotional/story arc ahead. This blow-by-blow account is visceral, it makes you want to wince. The only internal dialogue is, "But he was alive." Where another writer *using deep POV throughout the novel* might widen the lens and use a shallower point of view to show an out-of-body experience or use a summary technique to force the reader to lean in, Deon Meyer has zoomed way in to create the same but opposite effect for readers.

Be intentional about this. What effect are you trying to create?

Deep POV isn't difficult, but it does require a shift in how you think about writing. It will take practice, so be sure to find a critique partner who understands this technique and can help you find the gaps in internal dialogue, where telling has slipped in, or POV breaks. Find a great beta reader who's not a reader. When they're done reading, ask them pointed questions about their perception of the POVC's motives or goals at key points in the story. Their honesty will help you improve your story, so be sure to find someone who's willing to tell the truth (but someone kind enough to offer the criticism in a helpful way).

On my blog, you'll find other resources on writing fiction and some great archives on writing in deep point of view. Make sure you subscribe to the blog to get new posts in your inbox. If you're looking for support and encouragement on your writer's journey, join me on Facebook at the Confident Writers page. There's a closed group where I share lots of tips and inspiration for your day as well as conversation starters and story prompts to help you connect and network with other writers.

Thanks for reading! I hope this little book was helpful. The best way to thank a writer for their work is to write a review on whichever online retailer you purchased this book from, and of course tell all your writer friends how much you loved it.

Dive Deep!

Lisa

ACKNOWLEDGMENTS

From *The Silver Linings Playbook* by Matthew Quick, copyright ©2008 by Matthew Quick, published by Sarah Crichton Books, an imprint of Farrar, Straus and Giroux.

From *Cry Wolf* by Patricia Briggs, copyright ©2008 by Patricia Briggs, published by Hurog, Inc, an imprint of Penguin Group (USA) Inc.

From *The Last Seers* by Lisa Hall-Wilson, copyright ©2018 by Lisa Hall-Wilson, published by Lisa Hall-Wilson.

From *Ender's Game* by Orson Scott Card, copyright ©1999 by Orson Scott Card, published by Tor Teen Books, an imprint of Tom Doherty Associates, LLC.

From *Game of Thrones* by George R. R. Martin, copyright ©1996 George R. R. Martin, published by Bantam Books, an imprint of Penguin Random House LLC.

From *The Help* by Kathryn Stockett, copyright ©2011 by Kathryn Stockett, published by Berkley Books, an imprint of the Penguin Group (USA).

CONTACT THE AUTHOR

There's a lot of information in this little book. I hope you found the explanations and brief examples helpful. If you're looking for more help or ongoing help, be sure to check out the Confident Writers page on Facebook (there's a free group there where I offer additional helps) as well as my blog.

If you have questions or comments, feel free to email me through my website.

For more information about Lisa, her classes, books, or availability to speak to writers, visit:

https://lisahallwilson.com

Novels By Lisa Hall-Wilson

The Watched

The Last Seers

29136781R00071

Made in the USA
Columbia, SC
20 October 2018